COUNTIES OF
SOUTHERN
MARYLAND

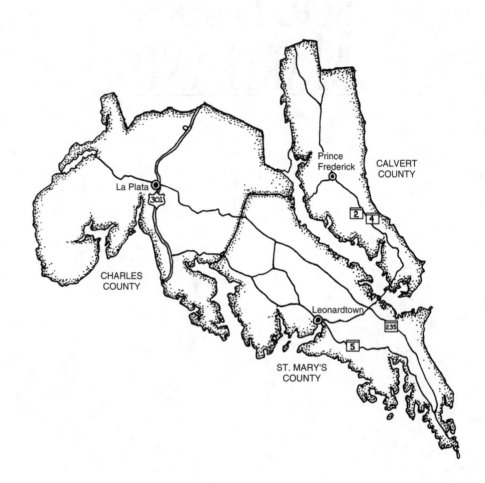

COUNTIES OF SOUTHERN MARYLAND

by Elaine Bunting & Patricia D'Amario

Tidewater Publishers

Centreville, Maryland

Library of Congress Cataloging-in-Publication Data

Bunting, Elaine
   Counties of Southern Maryland / by Elaine Bunting and Patricia
D'Amario.—1st ed.
      p. cm.—(Our Maryland counties series)
Includes bibliographical references (p.) and index.
Contents: Overview of Southern Maryland—Early Southern Maryland—
Revolutionary War—The War of 1812—Slavery, the Civil War, and
events that followed—The early twentieth century—The late
twentieth century—St. Mary's County (1637)—Calvert County (1654)
—Charles County (1658).
   ISBN 0-87033-535-9 (hardcover)
 1. Maryland, Southern—Juvenile literature. 2. Maryland,
Southern—History—Juvenile literature. 3. Maryland—History,
Local—Juvenile literature. 4. Saint Mary's County (Md.)—Juvenile
literature. 5. Calvert County (Md.)—Juvenile literature. 6. Charles
County (Md.)—Juvenile literature. [1. Maryland, Southern. 2. Saint
Mary's County (Md.) 3. Calvert County (Md.) 4. Charles County (Md.)] I.
D'Amario, Patricia. II. Title. III. Series: Bunting, Elaine.
Our Maryland counties series.
 F181.3 .B865 2002
 975.2'4—dc21

                                                                2002003432

Manufactured in the United States of America
First edition

To all my colleagues in the teaching profession and the field of library science, with whom I have worked over the years.

—E.B.

To my husband Jim, whose love, support, and encouragement are always with me.

—P.D.

CONTENTS

COUNTY SEALS

St. Mary's County
The seal of St. Mary's County has two lions standing on their hind legs with their front paws touching the state coat of arms. The Latin motto, *fatti maschii parole femine,* is the same as Maryland's and means "manly deeds, womanly words." It is thought the seal was first used in 1637.

Calvert County
The seal of Calvert County was designed for the county's three hundredth anniversary in 1954. The tobacco leaf on the seal represents the county's leading product. Fertility and hospitality are shown as a horn of plenty. The oyster shell represents the large supply of seafood in the county, and the rope and anchor symbolize its continuing nautical focus.

Charles County
A number of seals were used by Charles County before the present one was adopted. It was designed by Frederick Tilp, who used the Great Seal of Maryland as a starting point. The mother of the first Lord Baltimore is acknowledged by the red and white cross symbolizing the Crossland family coat of arms. The county was officially established in 1658.

PREFACE

In 1634, Father Andrew White arrived on the shores of the southern Maryland region in what is now St. Mary's City. Many of the people who came with him from Europe were seeking religious freedom. In their native country of England, they were not permitted to worship the way they wanted.

Their story is really Maryland's story, for St. Mary's is where the state began.

We would like to thank all the wonderful people who helped us when we were researching this book.

In St. Mary's County: Thank you to the staff of the St. Mary's County Public Library in Leonardtown, particularly Lois Coryell; Janet Cook, St. Mary's Chamber of Commerce; Judy Davies, County Commissioners Office; Michelle Morsell, District Court of St. Mary's County; Quentin Simpson and Mark Muir, Forest Service; Sergeant Myers, Maryland State Police, Leonardtown; Bleeker Harrison, Executive Secretary of St. Mary's County Historical Society; Deputy Delozier, St. Mary's County Sheriff's Department; Bert Bowling, Office of Economic and Community Development; and Karen Stanford, Public Relations, St. Mary's City.

In Calvert County: Thank you to the staff of the Calvert County Public Library in Prince Frederick, particularly reference librarian Pamela Perrygo, community services librarian Shirley McCarthy, and circulation supervisor Martha Mackall. Thank you also to Deputy Bragunier at the Circuit Court of Calvert County; Carolyn McHugh and Katie Crane, Calvert County Chamber of Commerce; Ruthie Buckler, Office of Economic Development; Richard Gould, Calvert

Marine Museum; Jane Coffin, artist; and Ailene W. Hutchins and Ann Whisman, Calvert County Historical Society.

In Charles County: Thank you to the staff of the Charles County Public Library in La Plata, particularly reference librarians Louise C. Crouse and Leigh Batty; Joanne Roland, Tourism Director for Charles County; Karen Cashill Lee, Steve Andritz, and Lacie Walter, Department of Planning and Growth Management; Nina W. Voehl, Public Information Officer for Charles County; Holbert Fazenbaker, docent at One-Room Schoolhouse in Port Tobacco; Terry Goss, docent at Port Tobacco Courthouse; Wayne Winkler, President of the Historical Society of Charles County, and Paula Winkler and Kathryn C. Newcomb, also with the historical society.

COUNTIES OF SOUTHERN MARYLAND

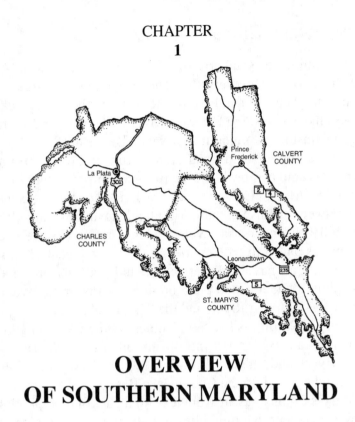

OVERVIEW
OF SOUTHERN MARYLAND

The history of Maryland began in the southern part of the state. On March 25, 1634, the first European settlers came to the area in hopes of finding religious freedom and economic opportunities. This group, led by Leonard Calvert, first landed on an island in the Potomac River and then settled on the mainland. The seat of Maryland's government also started here when the Maryland General Assembly first met in 1635. Today this southern area consists of three counties: St. Mary's (established in 1637), Calvert (1654), and Charles (1658).

Maryland is the only state in the United States that has a Calvert County, a Charles County, or a St. Mary's County. However, there is a Charles City County in Virginia, a Charles Mix County in South Dakota, and a St. Mary County in Louisiana. *FUN FACT*

Geography and Climate

The three counties of southern Maryland are located on the Atlantic Coastal Plain so they are very flat. They are lined with creeks which empty into the Patuxent and Potomac Rivers and the Chesapeake Bay. The Bay to the east and the Potomac River to the west and south form the large peninsula of southern Maryland. To the north of this region are Prince George's County and Anne Arundel County. Within the southern Maryland peninsula are the two smaller peninsulas of Calvert County and St. Mary's County which are divided by the Patuxent River flowing between them. Southern Maryland elevations range from sea level to 200 feet above sea level. Streams and creeks are deep and broad. Charles and Calvert Counties as well as the central part of St. Mary's County all have well-defined upland plateaus surrounded by low, flat plains. The lowland plain borders the Potomac River and its tributaries, the Patuxent River, and the Chesapeake Bay.

St. Mary's County is located 35 miles south of Washington, D.C. It has a land area of 373 square miles with soil of sand, clay, and gravel. Its many rivers and streams, forming 297 miles of shoreline, flow southeast and empty into the Chesapeake Bay.

St. Mary's County has an average of 40 inches of precipitation (rain and snow) each year in a mild climate with an average temperature in the summer of 75.9 degrees and in the winter of 38.2 degrees.

Calvert County is Maryland's smallest county with a land area of 244 square miles. It is about 30 miles long and, at its widest point, only 9 miles wide. The Chesapeake Bay and the Patuxent River form the boundary of the county on three sides. Of the county's 209 miles of shoreline, 32 miles are along the Chesapeake Bay. Calvert and St. Mary's Counties are both peninsulas.

Calvert County's elevation varies from sea level to 120 feet above sea level.

NOT-SO-FUN FACT	Erosion is a big problem along the Bay coast. Calvert County loses between 2 and 6 feet of coastline a year in some places. However, in other places such as Flag Ponds, the beaches have widened.

The Patuxent River was little more than a muddy creek hundreds of millions of years ago. At that time, it flowed in an easterly direction toward what is now the Chesapeake Bay. Near the end of the dinosaur era, earthquakes caused the Piedmont Plateau to be lifted high above the level of the Coastal Plain. Because of the change in elevation, streams ran faster and cut through the rocky plateau to create deep, narrow gorges. The Patuxent began to flow with greater velocity, and it also shifted its course. It flowed in a more southerly direction to empty into the Bay at the present-day mouth of the river at Drum Point in Calvert County. Creeks such as Hunting Creek, Fishing Creek, Parker's Creek, and Battle Creek run through the county.

A ridge called Sunderland Terrace runs the length of Calvert County. Streams to the east of this ridge flow into the Chesapeake Bay while streams on the west flow into the Patuxent River. There are two other ridges in the county, the Talbot Terrace and the Wicomico Terrace. Over fifteen million years ago, during the Miocene Era, a shallow sea covered this area. Marine animals died and sank to the bottom of the sea into the sand and clay. When the water level dropped, these shells and fossils remained. Now people find these fossils and shells on the beaches and embedded in the limestone cliffs. The water rose and fell two more times since then, though the land was never again completely underwater. This process took place over millions of years. Today the terraces are up to120 feet above sea level.

Geologists say the water level is rising, making it seem that the southern Maryland peninsula is in the process of sinking again. *FUN FACT*

Calvert County has a mild climate with an average summer temperature of 75.2 degrees and average winter temperature of 38.1 degrees. Yearly precipitation is 41.5 inches.

Charles County has approximately 150 miles of shoreline and covers 502 square miles, 44 of which are water. Its slightly rolling land has forests, swamps, creeks, and wetlands. Its soil is composed mainly of gravel, sand, and clay deposits which have washed down from the hills of the Piedmont Plateau. Because of the lack of solid rock, erosion occurs easily. The elevation varies from sea level to 200 feet above sea level.

Charles County has a mild climate. The average summer temperature is 74.1 degrees and the average winter temperature is 36.3 degrees. The county's yearly precipitation is 42.62 inches, and its average growing season is 185 days.

FUN FACT: According to the diary of Lewis Sutton, a minister in Calvert County, winters in the 1800s were much more severe than they are now.

Fossils of Calvert County

Calvert County is one of the best locations in the United States to hunt for fossils. Sharks' teeth are a popular find, but shells and bones of prehistoric whales and other marine mammals as well as some land animals are also found. Calvert Cliffs State Park and Scientists' Cliffs are two of the best places to find fossils. The Calvert Cliffs extend a distance of more than thirty miles, from a little north of Chesapeake Beach to Drum Point.

Ten to twenty million years ago, during the Miocene era, sediments were deposited in the Calvert Cliffs area as the ocean alternately covered the land and then receded. Bones of animals, even whole skeletons of birds and whales, were buried beneath the silt. Over many thousands of years, layer after layer of these bones, shells, and sharks' teeth accumulated in this shallow shoreline area. Finally, the water withdrew completely and left the former sea bottom exposed, creating the cliffs.

FUN FACT: Maryland's state fossil shell, designated in 1984, is the *Ecphora quadricostata*, an extinct snail or gastropod. The fossil can be found at various places in Maryland including Miocene beds in southern Maryland.

Other fossils found in Calvert County over the years have included bones of wolves, bears, deer, porpoises, mako sharks, saltwater crocodiles, turtles, and a pelican-like bird that was about six feet tall.

Wildlife

The southern Maryland counties of **St. Mary's, Calvert,** and **Charles** have a wide variety of wildlife. Many common varieties of birds can be found there such as cardinals, crows, red-winged blackbirds, cowbirds, grackles, swans, geese, ducks, doves, quail, purple martins, ospreys, wild turkeys, great blue herons, seagulls, marsh wrens, seaside sparrows, willets, barred owls, downy woodpeckers, pileated woodpeckers, and bald eagles. Charles County has the second largest population of bald eagles in the state.

The mammals in the area include deer, foxes, raccoons, opossums, squirrels, skunks, muskrats, rabbits, groundhogs, chipmunks, meadow voles, beavers, otters, and rabbits.

Turtles can be found in southern Maryland. These include the common snapping turtle and the northern diamondback terrapin, which is the Maryland state reptile. The southern leopard frog and the salamander are two amphibians found in the area, along with snakes like water snakes and copperheads. Spiders and a large variety of other insects such as mosquitoes, flies, common skimmers, and water striders can also be found. Southern Maryland has a wide range of beautiful butterflies as well, such as monarch, swallowtail, and painted lady.

Water creatures are among southern Maryland's most important natural resources. Fish such as striped bass (rockfish), silver and white perch, croaker, chain pickerel, crappie, bluegill sunfish, redear sunfish, and hardhead can be caught off its shores. Sheepshead minnows, spots, mummichogs, flounders, and bluefish are also found. There are blue crabs, marsh crabs, Atlantic ribbed mussels, oysters, and clams. The Patuxent River is also home to sea horses, horseshoe crabs, and jellyfish.

FUN FACT: A life-sized model of the largest sturgeon ever caught in the Chesapeake Bay hangs in the Calvert Marine Museum in Solomons in Calvert County. It is 14 feet long.

Endangered animals and those becoming endangered include black ducks, redhead ducks, American shad, oysters, least terns, dwarf wedge mussels, narrow mouth toads, corn snakes, and coastal plain milk snakes.

FUN FACT: A tiny protozoa called *Noctiluca scintillans* lives in Maryland's waters. It gives off light with every movement of the water. This light is visible only at night.

Plants

St. Mary's, Calvert, and **Charles Counties** have a wide variety of trees, including over 50 species of hardwoods. There are deciduous trees such as hickory, willow, dogwood, southern red and white oak, black gum, red maple, sweet gum, sycamore, beech, tulip poplar, and yellow poplar. Many types of pines and holly can also be found, including loblolly and Virginia pines.

FUN FACT   The largest post oak and the largest eastern red cedar in Maryland are in the yard of Ailene W. Hutchins of Calvert County. The oldest yew tree in the United States stands on the grounds of Tudor Hall in Leonardtown in St. Mary's County. Some unusual names of trees in southern Maryland are pawpaw, scarlet haw, Hercules club, butternut, and pignut hickory.

Vines such as Virginia creeper, wild grape, trumpet vine, honeysuckle, and poison ivy grow in southern Maryland. Indian turnip, fox grape, and pipe are found here as are wildflowers such as Queen

Anne's lace, lady's slipper, black-eyed Susan, and daisies. There are also many bushes and shrubs such as mountain laurel, bayberry, and staghorn sumac. Marsh grasses such as cord grass, cattails, and high-tide bush grass grow along southern Maryland's shores while aquatic grasses such as horned pond weed grow beneath its waters.

EARLY SOUTHERN MARYLAND

Native Peoples

The Native Americans living in southern Maryland were Piscataways, part of the Algonquian nation. There were about a dozen tribes including the Anacostian, Choptico, Patuxent, Mattaponi, Mattawoman, Wicomico, and Yaocomico. All were led by a king called a tayak, who lived in what is now Prince George's County. The white settlers called him an emperor. It was from the tayak that Governor Leonard Calvert bought the first land of the Maryland colony.

NOT-SO-FUN FACT:	At the time of the settlement of St. Mary's, the tayak was a man named Wannis. Wannis was murdered later by his brother Kittamaquund who then became the tayak.

The Piscataways were peaceful farmers and hunters like other eastern woodland natives. They wore jewelry made of shells, animal teeth, and eagle talons. They also wore aprons of deerskin around their waists and deerskin mantles (loose sleeveless garments) over their shoulders. In the summer, small children wore no clothing.

These natives lived near streams, creeks, or rivers. Their permanent villages were built like stockades so the people could take cover in times of danger. Their homes, called witchotts, had no furniture. The Indians slept on mats woven from swamp grass and rushes, and these became very popular with the colonists. Even the governor himself bought some of the mats from the natives. The governor used his as floor coverings instead of as sleeping mats.

The Piscataways traveled in dugout canoes, which they also used to fish for sturgeon, herring, shad, clams, and oysters. These canoes were made from large trees cut down with stone axes, hollowed out with fire, and smoothed with stone scrapers.

The rivers were important to the natives who used the Patuxent and Potomac Rivers to hunt beavers and otters for their fur. The Susquehannock tribe used the Patuxent River as a route from which to invade the lower Chesapeake tribes such as the Mattaponi and other Piscataways.

The natives used materials from nature to make tools. Stones were made into axes and tomahawks, pieces of antler or bone were used for needles, and sharpened clamshells became knives. After the white settlers came, the natives traded beaver skins for European axes, hoes, and other metal tools. They used plant fibers to make baskets, and from clay they made bowls, pots, and pipes for smoking tobacco.

The Piscataways were farmers and grew a variety of fruits and vegetables such as corn, beans, pumpkins, and squash. They grew tobacco, but it was not the variety that would later be grown by the settlers, because it was bitter and strong. Men and boys also hunted. Because hunting was so important to survival, the boys practiced daily with their bows and arrows.

The natives built temporary homes in the hunting areas and evidently hunted almost anything that moved. Archaeologists digging in old villages have found bones of all kinds of animals and birds, even skunks!

The Piscataways were mostly peaceful and friendly to the settlers, although there were isolated conflicts. They did have enemies among the other native tribes in Maryland. The Susquehannocks, Nanticokes, and Senecas fought with the Piscataways over hunting grounds and the fur trade. The Piscataways were true friends of the settlers; they helped to protect the settlers from the more warlike tribes such as the Susquehannocks.

Exploration

In 1608, Captain John Smith explored the Chesapeake. He and a group of fourteen men sailed in a small boat up the Bay from Jamestown, Virginia. They explored rivers as they traveled. Captain Smith's first trip was cut short by a storm and illness among his men. His second trip took him all the way to the Susquehanna River at the northern part of the Bay.

Captain Smith kept a diary of his two trips and drew a very accurate map of the areas he explored. He was very impressed with the Bay and its rivers and praised them highly in his diary. Smith's record was probably a major reason why the Calverts chose this area to colonize.

Another man who came to know the area quite well at that time was Captain Henry Fleet. He traded for furs with the natives along the shores of the Patuxent and Potomac Rivers and took the furs to Virginia to sell. He was helpful to Leonard Calvert and the first colonists in communicating with the Yaocomico Indians at what became St. Mary's.

Conditions in Europe

There are different reasons why people would leave their homeland to sail on a tiny ship and go to a wild land that may be populated with unfriendly natives. Sometimes it is for adventure or for the dream of wealth. Sometimes it is for religious freedom or for better living conditions. European settlers came to the New World for all these reasons and more. Between 1550 and 1650, the population in England almost doubled, and there was a shortage of jobs. Many people were left homeless and hungry, and everyone faced the threat of disease and death. In addition to the physical hardships, some people were not permitted to worship as they wished. Due to these difficulties, many people were desperate to leave and find a new life elsewhere.

At this time, European kings decided to send people to the New World to establish colonies for their countries. The kings were hoping for wealth and power over rival countries. Sir Walter Raleigh and George Calvert, favored friends of England's King James I, received huge grants of land in the New World. These men found investors (people to financially support the colony) and colonists (people to settle in the New World). These people left Europe and settled all along what would become America's East Coast from New England to Florida.

The Calverts of England

The history of St. Mary's County and Maryland starts with two friends in England—King James I and George Calvert. (Calvert's friend, Sir Robert Cecil, introduced him to King James.)

George Calvert had received his education at Oxford University, and his knowledge and helpfulness impressed the king. In 1617, King James I knighted him, which meant he was then a nobleman. Calvert was given the title Baron of Baltimore, the first Lord Baltimore.

Most people would think that being a wealthy nobleman and a friend of the king would shield a man from problems. It did not. Calvert's family was fined at least fourteen times for not following the teachings of the Anglican Church, the Church of England. The Calverts were Catholic, and at that time their religion was not tolerated. This lack of religious freedom was the major reason why the Calverts wanted to leave England.

After the death of King James I, George Calvert served the next king, Charles I. Calvert was interested in leaving England and starting a colony in the New World. He first moved to Newfoundland in Canada. After a very hard winter, he left and sailed south. He stopped in Virginia and was impressed by what he saw there. He decided to ask King Charles I for a grant of land just north, along the beautiful bay Captain Smith had described. The king granted him the land on the condition that he pay the king one-fifth of any gold and silver found there.

FUN FACT King Charles I also wanted the Calverts to send him two native arrows every year to show allegiance to England. The arrows were delivered for a number of years, but no gold or silver was ever found.

Sadly, George Calvert did not live to see his colony begin. He died April 15, 1632. Because George Calvert died before officially taking ownership of the land, his son Cecil signed the charter—the document that transferred the land to him. This charter was very important and gave Cecil some of the powers of the king. He could appoint leaders for his new colony and start a militia to defend it against natives and other enemies. He could establish cities and towns, set up courts and churches, and tax the colonists. The charter gave him all the powers he needed to establish a colony in the New World.

Cecil began to search for investors who would help finance the colony. He found some wealthy gentlemen who were interested, and the Society of Jesus (the Jesuits) also helped Lord Baltimore. They chartered the merchant ship *Ark* for the trip to the New World. Accompanying *Ark* would be *Dove,* a cargo ship owned by the investors. It had a crew of seven.

Cecil Calvert planned his colony very carefully. He opened an office in London where he offered free land to anyone who would sign up to go to the Maryland colony. He wrote rules called Conditions of Plantation describing how much land people would get. This mostly depended on the size of the family and number of servants. He published these conditions in England to encourage people to come to the New World. He made sure he had workers of many kinds because they would be needed in the colony. These included blacksmiths, carpenters, and farmers, as well as religious leaders. Many were indentured servants, who agreed to work for an employer for four to seven years if the employer would pay their passage to the new colony. Many were educated and some had mastered a skill, but because of the job shortage in England, many people were unemployed. Three-fourths of the colonists came to the colony as indentured servants.

When people signed up to go, Cecil Calvert gave them a letter of instruction to help them when they arrived in the colony. It gave them instructions on a variety of subjects, from planting corn to conducting worship services.

It took eighteen months to organize. There were several delays, but finally Calvert had everyone he needed, and they began final preparations for the trip.

Despite the many months of preparation, Cecil Calvert decided to stay in England to protect his grant. It was being challenged by people who were upset that he had decided to settle close to the Virginia colony of Jamestown. Cecil sent his younger brothers Leonard and George Calvert with the colonists, appointing Leonard as governor.

Leaving England

On the morning of November 22, 1633, 140 people stood on a dock at Cowes, England. They were waiting to board *Ark* for the long trip to the New World. Their belongings were being loaded aboard the cargo ship, *Dove*.

The people were no doubt excited but also a little nervous about the trip. After all, it would take four months to get to the colony site. The size of the ships was probably rather frightening. *Ark* was 125 feet long and 32 feet wide. It was actually a large ship for its time. It was built of oak and could be used as a merchant ship or as a Royal Navy ship in time of war. Belowdecks it was very dark and damp since the ship leaked. People lived belowdecks and supplies were also stowed there so it was overcrowded. This made the voyage dangerous and uncomfortable.

Dove was 76 feet long and 17 feet wide. It was a cargo ship, but it also carried a few passengers. It could carry 45 tons of cargo. Some of the supplies brought along for the journey were beer, cheese, biscuits, water, dried meat, and wood for cooking.

The colonists also brought lemons to prevent scurvy, a disease caused by lack of vitamin C. It is believed that the wealthier colonists probably brought wheat flour, butter, and live chickens.

This voyage was not a trip to be taken by cowards, and all the people on the dock were very determined. There was the possibility of pirates or storms at sea, or the ship could run out of food or water. Many of the people, but not all, were going for religious freedom. Some were looking for land, some for gold, and some for adventure. None probably realized what a different life they would find.

The journey did not start well. Four days out from England a bad storm hit and *Ark* was separated from the smaller *Dove*. They had tried to stay close to help each other if needed. People on *Ark* could see *Dove*'s distress signal, but the waves were so high that they could not help. *Dove* disappeared and the people on *Ark* thought it had sunk. *Ark* continued on to Barbados. While in port to take on supplies for the remainder of the trip, they were thrilled to see *Dove* sail into the harbor. It was not lost at sea after all! It had returned to England to wait out the storm. Then it set sail again, accompanied by another larger ship. After leaving Barbados, the two ships visited several other islands including Martinique and St. Christopher's Island, and the British passengers traded with the natives.

The details of the journey from England to Barbados are known because one of the colonists kept a diary of the trip. He was Father Andrew White, one of the Jesuit priests. *Ark* encountered another storm and was also threatened by pirates before arriving in Barbados.

FUN FACT

The two ships sailed north from the Caribbean. They stopped in Virginia to deliver letters from the king to the governor of Virginia. Then they sailed up the Chesapeake Bay into the Potomac River and landed on St. Clement's Island.

Settlement by Europeans

The colonists reached St. Clement's Island on March 25, 1634. They did not want to remain on the island because it was not very large, so Governor Leonard Calvert and a few other colonists sailed farther up the river to make contact with the natives. They looked for a better place on the mainland. They took with them Captain Henry Fleet who had been trading with the natives and knew their language This small scouting group discovered the native town, a Yaocomico village, that would become their home. They were relieved to find that the Indians were friendly. After returning to St. Clement's Island, they thanked God for their safe journey and erected a wooden cross on the island. This date, March 25, is celebrated today as "Maryland Day." For his help, Captain Fleet was given the first land grant of 2,000 acres.

Governor Calvert wanted to be fair with the natives, so on March 27, he bought land from the king of the Yaocomicos for his settlement.

According to Father White, the colonists decided to call their settlement St. Maries, in honor of the Virgin Mary. The spelling was eventually changed to St. Mary's. This settlement was the fourth permanent British settlement in North America. Later, the town was called St. Mary's City.

The natives were planning to leave the area anyway, because they were afraid of their enemies, the Susquehannocks. The colonists were able to move into the native village, which was on high ground. Huts were already built, the fields were ready to plant, and fresh water was nearby. It worked out very well for the colonists and for the natives too.

The first two buildings erected by the colonists were a storehouse and a guardhouse. Then the people unloaded *Ark* and *Dove* and began to live on the land rather than on the crowded ships. A stockade, or fence enclosure, was built to protect the village from the warlike Susquehannocks. The stockade was never needed because the warrior natives did not come. The colonists began to plant seeds for crops.

During the 1640s, the colonists did have problems with the Susquehannocks from Pennsylvania. They considered southern Maryland to be part of their hunting grounds, and they threatened homes and farms. Families were murdered and homes were burned. These Indians were using guns and knives that they had taken from Europeans. Governor Calvert helped the settlers in putting down the Indians and restoring peace to the colony.

Trouble in the Colony

Leonard Calvert did a very good job of leading the colony. He was a fair and honest man, and he was dedicated to religious freedom for all. Over the years the colonists claimed their land and built plantations small and large. More people came from England and settled other parts of Maryland. The Jesuit priests ministered to the colonists and to the natives.

The colony was not problem-free, however. In the early 1630s, a young Englishman named William Claiborne decided he was not going to honor the Calverts' ownership of Kent Island, which was located farther up the Chesapeake Bay from St. Mary's. In 1637, the Calverts forced him to leave both Kent and Palmer's Island in the Susquehanna River. Until 1652, Claiborne continued to claim these islands were his.

Another problem arose in 1642, when a man named Richard Ingle was arrested at St. Mary's for speaking against the king. He was able to escape and go back to England. He returned later with two heavily armed ships and captured the colony. Many of the colonists, including the governor, fled to Virginia. Father Andrew White and Father Thomas Copley were captured and taken back to England. In 1645, Ingle's men destroyed many official records. In 1646, Governor Calvert raised a force of men to go to St. Mary's and retake the colony, which they did without difficulty.

The colony also had trouble with Puritans who had come to Maryland to enjoy religious freedom but who would not tolerate the religious practices of others. Maryland was one of the few places where religious freedom was guaranteed by law. The Maryland General Assembly passed an Act of Religious Toleration in 1649 which said that religions of all people who believed in Jesus Christ were accepted. But the Puritans wanted everyone to worship their way, and there were violent confrontations between the Puritans and the other colonists.

Governor Leonard Calvert died in June 1647. Cecil Calvert named Thomas Greene to be the next governor, only to replace him in 1649 with a Protestant governor, William Stone, in hopes of pleasing the Puritans, who were trying to take the colony. Puritans governed England at this time, led by a man named Oliver Cromwell. In 1654, they took the colony away from the Calverts. Documents and papers relating to the colony were taken from St. Mary's. The Puritan Assembly met at "Preston at Patuxent," the plantation belonging to Richard Preston, located in what would become Calvert County. Lord Baltimore finally lost patience waiting to regain his colony and ordered Governor Stone to retake the colony any way he could. In 1655, a band of men supporting Stone attacked the plantation. The raiders recovered the documents and papers. During this raid the Great Seal of Maryland disappeared and was never found. It is possible that the seal may be found someday, either buried on the property or hidden behind a wall in the house.

Governor Stone then set sail for New Providence on the Severn River to try to take that town from the Puritans who had settled there. Stone landed at New Providence on March 25, 1655, and fought the Puritans in a battle that has become known as the Battle of the Severn. The Puritans beat Governor Stone's men, and the governor was wounded and taken prisoner. Meanwhile, Cecil Calvert worked hard to convince the Puritan government in England to give Maryland back to him. In 1658, he succeeded. Oliver Cromwell, the leader of England, returned the colony to the Calverts. Cecil immediately reinstated the Act of Religious Toleration so all people could worship freely.

A Royal Colony

In 1661, Charles Calvert, another son of Cecil, became governor of the colony. Charles is remembered for dividing the Eastern Shore into counties. By 1674, there were ten counties in Maryland: Anne Arundel, Baltimore, Calvert, Charles, and St. Mary's on the western shore of the Bay, and Dorchester, Somerset, Kent, Talbot, and Cecil on the Eastern Shore.

In 1689, the Calverts ran into trouble with their old enemies, the Puritans, also known as Protestants. In July, a group of Protestants called the Associators attacked St. Mary's City. They took over the State House. People loyal to Lord Baltimore tried to fight back, but they did not have enough support from other colonists. The Associators were supporters of King William and Queen Mary of England. King William appointed Sir Lionel Copley to be Maryland's first royal governor. Religious freedom again vanished, but some good things did happen under the royal government. Another royal governor, Francis Nicholson, moved the capital from St. Mary's City to Anne Arundel Town. This small town was more central to the colony and easily accessible from the Severn River. St. Mary's City was very far south and hard to reach. The roads were poor and there were many rivers and streams to cross. Soon afterward, the name of the new capital was changed to Annapolis which means "city of Anne." The city was named for Princess Anne who later became Queen Anne. Annapolis has remained the capital of Maryland ever since. In 1994, Annapolis celebrated its three hundredth anniversary as the state capital.

NOT-SO-FUN FACT

In 1667, a hurricane hit Maryland. It was evidently one of the worst in history. Colonists reported hail the size of turkey eggs, about three inches long and two and a half inches wide. Strong winds destroyed homes and barns. The hail killed livestock and many wild animals. That year's crop of tobacco was lost.

During the royal rule, education received a boost from a law passed by the General Assembly in 1694. According to this law, whenever furs or animal skins were exported from Maryland, part of the money from taxes on these went to education. The act also established the first free school in Annapolis. It became St. John's College, which is still in existence today.

Another improvement that came from the royal government was the establishment of the first postal route from St. Mary's City to Philadelphia, Pennsylvania. This was a distance of about 200 miles. If a colonist in St. Mary's City sent a letter to a friend in Philadelphia, the letter would arrive in about two weeks. This seems slow today, but it was a big improvement at the time.

In 1715, the ownership of the Maryland colony was returned to the Calverts. Benedict Calvert gave up Catholicism, which pleased King George I. The years before the American Revolution saw much growth in the colony. The population more than tripled due to the immigration of many people from European countries such as Germany, Ireland, Italy, and France. There was also an increase in the number of slaves brought into the colony. By 1760, slaves made up one-third of Maryland's population.

FUN FACT   One reason why Maryland's population grew was because a family might have as many as ten or twelve children.

Settlement of the Southern Counties

Although many historic events in the area relate to the settlement of the Maryland colony at St. Mary's, records have established that **St. Mary's County** existed as early as 1637. The population grew as many settlers came from England for the opportunity to escape poverty and own land. As more people established plantations, there was a need for more help to grow tobacco. Indentured servants worked for several years, but once freed, they started their own plantations. So there was a continuing need for additional labor. By the 1650s, slaves were being brought to the colony. Their numbers increased over the years as plantations grew larger and more numerous.

By the 1680s, St. Mary's City had a chapel, a State House, and a prison. Homes and other buildings were built along roads through the town. Historians thought that there was no plan to the town Governor Calvert started to build. However, archaeologists digging at St. Mary's found that the settlement was in the shape of two triangles. The prison and the chapel were equally distant from the town center. The State House also served as an inn or "ordinary" to help pay for its expenses.

Settlers who came to what is now **Calvert County** migrated from the St. Mary's area and spread along the Patuxent River. At the time, this area was still part of St. Mary's County. Soon after the first colonists came on *Ark* and *Dove,* Quakers (Society of Friends), Huguenots, and Scotsmen settled along the Patuxent River and St. Leonard's Creek. This was recorded in the minutes of the Maryland General Assembly in 1642. During the next fifty years the area's population grew steadily.

Taverns were known as "ordinaries" because ordinary people could go there to eat and drink. It was found that drinking and running the government did not mix, so in 1767, a new, brick State House was built. The old State House continued to serve as an ordinary.	*FUN FACT*

Puritans were also among the early settlers of the county. Many of them came from Virginia because they did not agree with the rule of the Virginia governor. They left Virginia and moved north in 1649 to the area that has become Anne Arundel County. By 1651, they were also settling in what is now Calvert County.

There was some settlement along the Chesapeake Bay side of the county, but not as much as on the Patuxent side because of the high cliffs along the shoreline. There were no natural harbors and people would have to climb a long way to the top of the cliffs.

The settlers hunted for salt along the cliffs. They used it to preserve their food.	*FUN FACT*

The Patuxent River and its streams were deep enough for ships and provided easy transportation and docking for ships and boats. The land along the Patuxent is fertile and well suited for agriculture. So it was a natural choice for the settlers.

Settlement by colonists in **Charles County** occurred mostly from 1649 to 1660. During this period, the Native Americans disappeared due to advances by the colonists. The settlers did not pay the Indians for this land. They did not recognize that the Indians owned it because Lord Baltimore had given the colonists this land. Earliest settlement in what is now Charles County was along the Wicomico River and its valley. Settlement spread to the Port Tobacco River, the Nanjemoy Creek, and Mattawoman Creek. Lord Baltimore granted large tracts of land which were eventually divided into smaller manors. Political divisions of the original manors were called "hundreds." Some of these hundreds were named Pykawaxen Hundred, Riverside Hundred, Chicamuxen Hundred, and Nanjemoy Hundred.

Homes

When the settlers first came to Maryland, they lived in the native village Governor Calvert bought. The Yaocomicos lived in huts called wigwams or witchotts, which they built by placing tall tree branches into the ground in two rows. Then they tied the branches together and covered the top with animal hides or thatch. Some settlers built homes similar to these and added chimneys for fireplaces. These chimneys were not built of bricks. They were made of wood covered with clay. The clay would harden and the chimney would be good for a few years. Colonists had to watch them closely though, for eventually the clay would crack and fall out. If this happened and the chimney was not repaired quickly, a fire could start. There is no stone found in this region so the settlers' early homes must have been built of wood, brick, and clay.

FUN FACT   In 1664, the St. Mary's City Assembly passed a law which was Maryland's first building code. It declared that all homes built in the town had to be at least 20 feet square and 2½ stories high. They were to have brick chimneys.

Early roofs were made of thatch, which consisted of straw or branches. However, the Maryland settlers thatched their cabin roofs with heavy vines such as Virginia creeper or reeds. The thatch was put on in thick layers on the frame of the roof to keep out rain and snow. These cabins were just one room. The oiled paper windows were not clear, but they let in some light. Inside, there were doors like shutters that were closed over the windows at night. The door to the house was heavy, and a strong wooden bar was put over it at night for safety.

At first the small and midsize farmhouses were made of wood. These might last about twenty years, at which time dampness and termites made them unlivable. As soon as a family could afford to do so, a brick house was built.

Many people made their own furniture, cups, plates, candles, and clothes. If the family was fortunate, eventually it would be able to order furniture, clothes, and other items from England. These were paid for with tobacco. They were brought to the colonies on ships that had taken tobacco to England from Maryland.

When making clothes for the colonists, a tailor in London would have to guess the person's size because the colonist was not there to try on the clothes as they were being made. So the colonists' nicest clothes rarely fit properly. Everyday clothes were sewn by a person's mother or by a servant or slave, so they fit better. These were called "homespun" and were made of wool or linen.

FUN FACT

Many of the people who started small farms in the area had been indentured servants. Almost half of the people that made up Maryland's population by the mid-1600s were, or had been, indentured servants. They worked hard and some of them became wealthy.

Tobacco was a very important crop to the settlers because it was used as money. However, tobacco uses up the nutrients in the soil, and eventually crops become poorer and poorer. If a colonist did well with his crops, he might buy the farm next door or another piece of land elsewhere. In this way, he added to his holdings and had more land to plant tobacco.

Some colonists wanted to use all their land to plant tobacco. However, Lord Baltimore realized this could lead to a shortage of food for the colonists. He made a law that every farm and plantation must plant at least two acres of corn for every person living there. Fish and corn were staples of the colonists. Unlike today, very few people raised cattle.

As soon as possible, a colonist would add outbuildings to his plantation. These were buildings such as storehouses, a smokehouse (to preserve meat), a tobacco barn, a tool house, and several cabins. Some of these cabins were homes for slaves, if the planter had enough tobacco to buy them. Some were for indentured servants or freemen. The indentured servants worked to repay their passage to the colony; freemen were paid.

FUN FACT	Nails were handmade and very hard to get. When a colonist needed a new house or other building, he often burned the old one down. He then searched through the ashes for the nails.

When the family could afford to do so, they built a larger, brick home with a shingle roof. Because of the danger of fire, the kitchens in these nicer homes were sometimes built separate from the main two-story house. The largest room downstairs was called "the hall." It held the fireplace, a table and chairs, a wooden bench, a linen chest, and perhaps an armchair for the head of the family. Some homes had a parlor (a small living room) downstairs, but it was reserved for guests. Upstairs were two bedrooms. Pegs on the wall were used to hang clothes because there were no closets. The beds were feather mattresses supported by ropes.

Children slept in the attic or loft on pallets (beds of straw or rags). The youngest children slept on trundle beds in their parents' bedroom. These were low to the floor and could be pushed under their parents' bed during the day.

Life on a Tobacco Plantation

People in colonial times could grow their own money. Tobacco was used for money, and most farms of that time grew it. (Some coins were also used for money in the colonies.) Today people know that smoking tobacco can be very bad for their health, but the colonists and the Native Americans did not know that—neither did people in Europe. Europeans enjoyed smoking tobacco, and they paid coin money for it. Naturally, colonists grew as much tobacco as they could because coin money was scarce. They used tobacco to buy salt and sugar, as well as to pay for land, rents, taxes, and other things. Hired help was also paid in tobacco that was measured by the pound.

Tobacco seeds were planted in the spring. The type of tobacco grown was called oronooko, a South American variety. The tobacco grown by the natives was very bitter. It had to be mixed with other things to be mild enough to smoke, so the colonists did not grow it.

Tobacco seeds are so small that a tiny stack of seeds only ¼-inch high can sow 100 square yards of a field. One tablespoon can hold about 85,000 seeds.   ***FUN FACT***

Near the end of July, when the tobacco plants were over six feet tall, the flowers were pinched off to make the leaves grow bigger. In August, the plants were cut down and draped across long sticks that were hung side by side in the tobacco barn or on a fence to allow the tobacco to dry. Tobacco barns were wooden buildings with gaps in the walls. Air could flow through and dry the tobacco. Drying took about six weeks and turned the leaves from green to brown. The tops were then cut off the plants and the seedpods were stored until planting time the following spring. The leaves were pulled off the plant, tied together in flat bunches, and stored over the winter in the barn. (Growing tobacco is a long process. These are only the main steps.)

When the tobacco was ready for market it was put into huge wooden barrels called "hogsheads." One of these could hold between 400 and 500 pounds of tobacco. Hogsheads varied in size between 1658 and 1872 as the government attempted to establish a standard size. In 1872 hogsheads were standardized to 54 inches high and 48 inches across.

The wooden hogsheads were built on the plantation. When full of tobacco, they were so heavy they had to be rolled to warehouses along "rolling roads." The warehouses were located near a wharf where the tobacco was loaded onto ships for the trip to England (or to one of several other countries). Some of the tobacco was kept at the plantation to be used as money.

Tobacco was shipped to Europe in huge convoys (groups of ships). Sometimes between 150 and 200 ships sailed down the Chesapeake Bay to the Atlantic Ocean. Convoys provided protection at sea from enemy ships and privateers. The Dutch were considered to be a major enemy. In the mid-1600s, they entered the Bay and attacked ships. Since tobacco was used as money, the tobacco trade was very important to the British government. They eventually allowed tobacco ships to sail only in convoys, and only one convoy would sail each year. In 1707 it was decided the convoy would reach the Bay in October and leave for England in May so it would miss the bad weather at sea. Although this worked very well, there were problems finding crews for the ships. By the early 1700s, half the tobacco crop of Maryland and Virginia was sitting in warehouses due to the rising cost of shipping it. The tobacco was good for only a few months, so it could not be saved for the following year when the convoy left again.

By 1750, 72 million pounds of tobacco were produced in the Chesapeake area annually.

Early County Government

The earliest governments in St. Mary's, Calvert, and Charles Counties were manorial—the plantations were self-governing, even holding court handling legal matters and trying people accused of crimes.

As counties were established, courts were convened. These courts were the center of county government in St. Mary's, Calvert, and Charles Counties. Justices or commissioners of the courts oversaw the running of the counties. These men were appointed by the governor. They held trials and levied taxes to pay for roads and ferries, and appointed other officers such as constables and road supervisors.

The High Sheriff, appointed by the governor, was the law-enforcing officer. He was also in charge of holding elections at the courthouse. The election districts in the early counties were called hundreds. Each hundred had a constable who enforced laws and was under the control of the High Sheriff.

For a number of years following the settlement of St. Maries (as it was spelled then), the provincial and the St. Mary's County governments were closely entwined. Soon after settling, Lord Baltimore set up a provincial government of two commissioners and an assembly of freemen in the colony led by himself. This assembly was eventually divided into an "upper" house of the governor and a council and a "lower" house of elected representatives from the counties. The assembly established a provincial court and a county court. These courts met in St. Mary's at the same time and some men served on both. The total separation of the St. Mary's County and the Maryland provincial governments did not happen until around 1655, when the county court was moved to Newtown Hundred near Leonardtown.

Establishment of Towns

Towns were slow to be established in southern Maryland because people preferred to live on their farms and plantations. Lord Baltimore granted large tracts of land to people. A planter's wealth was determined by the amount of land he owned. People were more interested in acquiring additional land than they were in owning a house in a town. Life was quite different for the Puritans in New England. They depended on fishing and businesses and therefore settled in towns. Small towns eventually did grow in southern Maryland. The Maryland General Assembly passed an act in 1683 for "the Laying out of Towns." Many towns grew up along creeks and rivers because these were places from which to ship tobacco. Each town appointed a man to collect taxes. Eventually, when paths were cleared through the forests, people moved further inland. By the 1800s, a typical town had a blacksmith shop, a harness shop, one or more general stores, mills, churches, and a foundry where metal tools and hardware were made. A wheelwright shop (wagon wheel maker) and warehouses for tobacco were also located in the towns. Some towns, such as Chaptico in St. Mary's County, were ports of entry and had customhouses which were business offices for shipping. Other towns were named in honor of prominent people, such as Leonardtown, established in 1660. Some towns, such as Port Tobacco in Charles County, were built on the sites of former Indian villages. Others grew up around large businesses such as the cannery at Solomons in Calvert County.

Establishment of Roads and Transportation

Transportation routes in the early days of the colony were similar throughout the southern Maryland area. During the earliest days, there were no roads, just trails through the forest. When people wanted to travel, they usually went by water, so they settled along the rivers and streams. Since there were few carriages, roads were not a top priority. The rivers and even some streams, such as Hunting Creek and Battle Creek in Calvert County, were very deep, and even seagoing sailing ships could navigate them.

The lack of roads and bridges created problems in early Maryland. Some of the first delegates to the Maryland General Assembly could not get to St. Mary's City because they could not cross the St. Mary's River (then called the St. George's River).

Roads on land were not highways. In southern Maryland there were private roads leading from the tobacco barns to the river landings. These were the rolling roads that were used to move hogsheads of tobacco. "Wood roads" were paths through the woods that had been cleared in order to haul firewood and building timbers from the forest to the plantation. Eventually these became bridle paths for horses, and they were linked together.

FUN FACT Paths were so narrow that travelers carried axes when they were in the forest. If two wagons approached each other from opposite directions, the travelers had to cut away a clearing to pass each other.

Eventually, better roads were needed. The first public road in **St. Mary's County** was called Mattapany Path and was built sometime before 1639. It still exists today. Now called Mattapany Road, it connects Routes 5 and 235.

An important early road in **Calvert County** was a north and south route called the Ridge Road or the Severn Path. This road intersected a road that led from Calvertown to the cliffs. This was the primary intersection of the county and later became the center of Prince Frederick. Another important road was the Dividing Path. It was called this because on one side of the road water flows toward the Patuxent River, and on the other side it flows toward the Bay.

In **Charles County** the Potomac River was the first "roadway." Because there were no actual roads, colonists used rivers to travel from place to place.

The Wicomico River divides part of Charles County into two sections. In 1658, an act was passed to establish a ferry to cross the river. This enabled people to travel easily between the two shores.

In 1695, a post route was established from the Potomac River through Annapolis to Philadelphia. Although the colony had a post road, people did not get their mail regularly. In 1704, a law was passed creating a system of highways throughout southern Maryland. These roads were 20 feet wide. Today, a two-lane road is 24 feet wide.

More roads were built including one connecting Charles County with St. Mary's and one from northern St. Mary's County to Point Lookout, the southernmost point in the state. These roads were dirt and were probably extremely muddy at times and had many ruts as well. The 1704 legislation also provided for overseers to take care of the roads, and to be sure they were cleared of debris. The overseers had the power to summon men to work on the roads. Anyone who refused was fined.

A number of county roads were built during the 1800s. These were maintained by road supervisors who made sure they were kept in good condition for carriages, carts, and wagons. In 1868, the office of County Superintendent of Roads was established in St. Mary's County.

Until 1910, the only important roads in Charles County led to ferry landings, river docks, and railroad stations. The completion of roads and bridges helped many towns to develop. For example the Potomac River Bridge, built in 1940, contributed to the growth of Waldorf and La Plata in Charles County. It was renamed the Harry W. Nice Memorial Bridge in 1967 for Governor Nice, who served from 1935 to 1939.

During the 1800s and early 1900s, large steamboats carried passengers and freight up and down the Bay. One early line was the Washington-Alexandria-Georgetown Steamboat Packet Line with its steamers *Frederick, Columbia,* and *Franklin.* Later *Baltimore* and *Maryland* were added. Another was the Weems Steamboat Line, which was the longest running line in the U.S., in continuous use from the 1820s to about 1900. These steamboats were large and had several decks. They were very grand looking, but were actually very economical. They had staterooms for overnight trips and were a comfortable way to travel. During the steamboat era, there were more than three hundred landings in the Chesapeake Bay area.

While steamboats were very popular in the 1800s, steamboat travel declined in the 1920s because automobiles were invented. Many people also traveled by train. Some of the steamboat lines were bought by the Pennsylvania Railroad. The company considered the railroad lines to be more important than the steamboat line.

Railroads

Before the railroads most people traveled by horse-drawn buggies, wagons, or stagecoaches. Road travel was dangerous and had many problems. Stagecoaches overturned, the roads were muddy, and many people were robbed. Early railroads had a smoother ride, but they were no faster. There were no engines. Horses pulled the cars along the rails. The invention of the steam engine in England in the early 1800s improved rail travel there, but these improved railroads did not appear in the United States until the late 1820s.

Railroads in **St. Mary's County** were a disappointment to county residents who had hoped for a line to link the county wharves with railroad lines going to other parts of the state and country. It never happened. A line was built from Brandywine to Mechanicsville and went into service in 1881. This was the Southern Maryland Railroad. The line was sold several times over the years. Eventually local citizens bought it. It became known as the "Farmer's Railroad." In 1942, construction began on the Naval Air Station Patuxent River, and the navy took over the Farmer's Railroad. They used it until 1954.

Three of the men who ran the Farmer's Railroad were actually farmers. They worked on the railroad two days a week, on their farms four days a week, and then took Sunday off.   *FUN FACT*

In **Calvert County,** a rail line was built into Chesapeake Beach by Otto Mears and David Moffat, railroad builders from Colorado. Mears had the idea to build a fancy resort on the Bay and bring wealthy vacationers from Washington, D.C. The railroad line was about 35 miles long and was called the "Honeysuckle Route." During the depression, the number of people vacationing in Chesapeake Beach dropped, and the rail line went out of business. During the late 1800s and early 1900s, efforts were made to build a rail line from Baltimore and Washington to Drum Point. It was thought that Drum Point could become an important harbor if it was connected by rail to large cities. However, lack of money kept the project from becoming a reality.

In **Charles County,** a line of the Baltimore and Potomac Railroad was opened in 1862. It ran to Pope's Creek and was called the Pope's Creek Branch. The Baltimore and Potomac Railroad did not build a main line into Washington, D.C. Instead, they built a main line into Pope's Creek, then built a branch line into Washington. Some people wanted to extend the line across the Potomac into Virginia, but this did not happen.

The Baltimore and Potomac Railroad came to Waldorf in 1872 and to La Plata in 1873. The railroad built a station, a telegraph office, and a store on the Chapman farm called La Plata. The town of La Plata later grew around the store.

REVOLUTIONARY WAR

The movement to separate from England was slow to reach southern Maryland, partly because of its distance from the other counties and partly because there was not as much resentment toward England. The British did not tax the southern counties as heavily as the rest of the colony because southern Maryland was selling large amounts of tobacco to Britain. The British warships protected the shipment of this tobacco to England.

For 131 years, the only "tax" the Maryland colonists had to pay to the king of England consisted of two native arrows, to be delivered every Easter Thursday. However, in 1765, England passed the Stamp Act, which placed a tax on many kinds of legal papers and other items.

FUN FACT   The Stamp Act put a tax on playing cards and college diplomas as well as calendars, newspapers, and dice.

The Stamp Act was later repealed (canceled), but England passed another set of acts at about the same time, and these also angered the colonists. These Townshend Acts taxed items imported into the colonies. These acts were also repealed eventually, except for the tax on tea. Most of the colonists were of English descent, and they drank a lot of tea. So they were very angry that the tax on tea was not repealed. On December 16, 1773, a group of colonists in Boston, Massachusetts, boarded a British ship loaded with tea. They dumped the 340 chests of tea into the harbor to let the government know they did not want the tea tax. St. Mary's County finally decided to let England know how it felt about the tea tax. In August of 1774, a ship loaded with tea was turned away. The captain was told no tax would be paid and no tea would be unloaded. This was about eight months after the Boston Tea Party.

People all over the colony of Maryland were slow to decide to go to war. After all, their ancestors were from England, and most still considered themselves English men and women.

People who did not agree that the colonists should fight were called "Tories" or "Loyalists" because they were loyal to England. People who wanted freedom from England were considered by the Tories to be rebels.

FUN FACT

Another reason people had trouble deciding whether or not to go to war concerned the man who was the governor at the time. Governor Robert Eden was very popular with the colonists. Though he tried very hard to settle differences between the Maryland colonists and the British Crown, he failed. After all, Maryland was not the only colony involved in the conflict. In June 1776, he gave up and sailed home to England.

As early as 1774, war committees were being formed in the counties. The Second Continental Congress met in Philadelphia and wrote resolutions asking the colonists not to import anything from England. The resolutions also required each county to form a militia and to provide weapons. The committee in **St. Mary's County** voted to approve these resolutions and to act on them. This is important because it shows that as many as two years before the war, St. Mary's County was preparing just in case.

In the summer of 1775 at the Maryland Convention, it was decided to establish two companies of "minutemen." The men were called this name because they could be ready to fight at a minute's notice. Each company was to have a captain, two lieutenants, an ensign, four sergeants, four corporals, a drummer, and a fifer. Each would have sixty-eight privates. These two companies from St. Mary's County were combined with companies from Charles County and Prince George's County to form a battalion. A colonel and a lieutenant colonel led the battalion. All men between the ages of sixteen and fifty were expected to serve.

When the Revolutionary War started, most people thought it would be a short war. When they realized that it would drag on longer than first expected, they reorganized the military units. There were two types of troops in the war: soldiers in the Continental Army organized by Congress and militia units organized by the colonies.

In July 1776, Congress created the Flying Camp Mobile Reserve Units made up of troops from Maryland, Delaware, and Pennsylvania. One of these, a unit led by John Allen Thomas from St. Mary's County, saw action on Maryland soil.

FUN FACT   The Flying Camp units did not really "fly," of course, since airplanes had not yet been invented.

On July 12, 1776, about four months after the start of the war, Colonel Richard Barnes spotted a fleet of British ships off Point Lookout. The fleet of about seventy ships must have frightened the colonists as it sailed up the Potomac River and anchored near St. George Island. The fleet was under the command of a former governor of Virginia, Lord Dunmore, who had been forced to leave Virginia because of his loyalty to England. There were also many loyalists from Virginia aboard the ships. Food and water were low and smallpox had broken out on the ships. (Smallpox is a terrible disease that causes blisters on the skin, and in most cases, death.)

The colonial militia under Captain John Allen Thomas responded to the shore opposite St. George Island and tried to drive the British away from the area. They were helped by conditions on board the ships, which were rapidly getting worse as many people died from the smallpox.

Since the British could not keep the bodies of the dead smallpox victims on board, they threw them overboard.

NOT-SO-FUN
FACT

Conditions on shore were bad for the militia as well. It was mid-July, so it was very hot and humid. A shortage of fresh water made it even more difficult. The militiamen were probably very glad to see the arrival of *Defense,* a Maryland ship with twenty-two cannons. *Defense* was not able to destroy the British fleet, but along with the militia it did discourage Lord Dunmore from setting up headquarters on St. George Island.

Near the end of the year, John Allen Thomas's unit was incorporated into the Continental Army.

During the war, a big problem in the county was a lack of weapons. In 1777, the army had more troops than it had guns to arm them. Another problem was the presence of British warships patrolling the water off St. Mary's County. They interfered with transportation of cargo. This was bad because St. Mary's County provided food such as fish, beef, flour, and bacon to American troops throughout the war. Shipments were sometimes delayed. British ships also harassed the colonists by firing on their homes from the water. Sometimes the British sailors came ashore and burned colonists' homes and businesses. They took food, horses, cattle, tobacco, and even slaves. Some colonists were taken prisoner. This harassment continued throughout the war.

Several men from St. Mary's County distinguished themselves in the navy during the Revolutionary War. Captain George Cook became commander of *Defense.* Twenty-four other men from St. Mary's County were already serving aboard the ship at that time.

Many others from St. Mary's joined the Maryland forces defending New York against the British. This group was known as the "Maryland Line." On August 27, 1776, these troops held off the British on Long Island until General George Washington's army could retreat to safety. Though outnumbered, they refused to surrender.

Another distinguished patriot from St. Mary's County was Major Abraham Barnes, who was active in resisting the taxes being charged the colonies. His son, Richard Barnes, served as a delegate to the Maryland Convention that elected men as representatives to the Continental Congress. In 1781, he assembled a group of boats owned by local people to carry some of General George Washington's army to Virginia. This was an important event because it enabled Washington to meet the French General Lafayette at Yorktown. The Battle of Yorktown was the last battle of the Revolutionary War. The armies of Washington and Lafayette defeated that of the British General Cornwallis and won the war for the Americans.

In 1774, landowners from **Calvert County** elected representatives to the Continental Congress. They supported the movement for separation from England even though England was a major market for their tobacco. Luckily, the Revolution did not affect the tobacco market.

On November 16, 1774, voting landowners of Calvert County adopted a three-part resolution to name the people who would represent them at the Continental Congress and the Provincial Convention in Annapolis. Many other counties also appointed committees to attend these meetings. This was to prepare for war with England and to raise money to buy weapons and supplies. Soon after, on April 24, 1775, the Maryland Convention in Annapolis adopted resolutions to boycott British goods and raise a militia.

The primary job of the militia in Calvert County was to protect the county from British invasion and to carefully watch for British warships in the Chesapeake Bay. In 1780 and 1781, the British burned many homes along the Patuxent River. Men from Calvert and Prince George's Counties formed an association to protect the river with fortifications. One of these was at Magruder's Landing in Prince George's County and one was at Hallowing Cliffs on the Patuxent River in Calvert.

Calvert County's leading patriot during the Revolutionary War was Thomas Johnson, who became the first governor of the State of Maryland. He was a lawyer who became an associate justice of the

U.S. Supreme Court. He was a member of the Continental Congress and he nominated George Washington to become the commander-in-chief of the Continental Army.

Another person from Calvert County who distinguished himself in the war was General James Wilkinson. He served in many battles including Saratoga, Princeton, and Trenton, eventually reaching the rank of Brigadier General.

In 1807, General James Wilkinson testified against Aaron Burr when Burr was tried on charges of treason. Washington Irving (author of *The Legend of Sleepy Hollow* and *Rip Van Winkle*) was at that time a newspaper reporter. He attended this trial and was struck at how conceited Wilkinson was. He mentioned him in his article and called him "General von Poffenberg."

FUN FACT

The people of **Charles County** were concerned about their civil rights because of the absentee landlordship practiced by Lord Baltimore in England. They were also upset with the way the Church of England operated in the colony. Even if a colonist was not a member of the Church, he was still expected to support the parish. Congregations were not allowed to choose their ministers. Instead, they were chosen by Lord Baltimore. As a result of these two issues, the colonists began to think about revolution. On January 1, 1776, the Maryland Convention appointed people including two Charles County men, Francis Ware and Thomas Stone, to collect clothing and gather troops to serve in the Maryland Line.

By June of 1776, the desire for independence from England became very strong. The county committee advised their delegates at the State Convention that they wanted the Maryland delegates at the Continental Congress to vote for separation from England. They also wanted them to establish a confederation of colonies.

Many Charles County men fought under General William Smallwood in the Maryland Line. Their first major battle was the Battle of Brooklyn in New York.

During the war Walter Hanson, Jr., and John Hanson, Jr., attempted to build a powder mill that would supply all the gunpowder the state of

Maryland would need during the war. This represented the first attempt at industry in Charles County. This mill was never completed because the men were needed to serve in the militia and the people they employed enlisted in the army.

In 1778, over two thousand men from Charles County proved their support of the movement for independence by signing the Oath of Allegiance to Maryland in which they gave up their allegiance to England.

British warships patrolled the Potomac River and raided towns and plantations along the river. They hoped to gain control of the Potomac to stop the flow of men and supplies through the colonies. This was unsuccessful because of the fierce resistance of the colonists.

The war ended with the Treaty of Paris, signed by Great Britain and America on September 3, 1783. Great Britain then recognized the thirteen original colonies as the United States of America. The newly elected members of the United States Congress in Annapolis then ratified (approved) the treaty which officially ended the war on January 14, 1784.

After the war, Maryland joined the United States of America by ratifying the newly written Constitution of the United States on April 8, 1788. It was the seventh state to do so.

During the years after the Revolutionary War, several thousand people from St. Mary's County and Charles County heard the call of the west. Many men were given land in Kentucky and other western states by the government for serving in the Continental Army during the war, but land out west was available to anyone. Some people moved for religious reasons. Catholics had not been allowed to hold political office in Maryland since the last part of the 1600s. Others went for economic reasons. The British had taken many possessions, the economy was poor, and people wanted to start over in a new place. During the time of this westward movement, the population of St. Mary's County dropped from 15,544 to 12,794.

In 1829, the Baltimore and Ohio Railroad was built from Baltimore westward. Many people from Calvert County moved to Ohio and other parts of the Midwest. After a financial panic and depression in 1837, more people left for a new start. During the early 1800s, the population of Calvert County dropped. During the mid-1800s, it remained virtually the same.

THE WAR OF 1812

After the Revolutionary War, Marylanders thought they had seen the last of war. However, another occurred thirty years later. The War of 1812 started in Europe as an economic dispute between Britain and France. It spread to Canada and America as Britain tried to preserve its ownership of Canada.

Even before the war, southern Maryland felt the effects of the problems with Britain. The counties were in very poor shape economically. In 1807, America passed an embargo, an act that closed American ports to all nations. The action was intended to hurt Britain and France, but it harmed America more. For instance, southern Maryland had large amounts of tobacco it could not sell or ship to other markets.

War between the United States and Great Britain was declared on June 18, 1812. Marylanders did not see any action until December 26 when the British blockaded the Chesapeake, preventing ships from entering or leaving the Bay. This was a disaster for economically depressed southern Maryland. The Bay was blockaded for two years, and at times only the clipper ships were able to get through. Due to their speed, they were able to outrun the British ships forming the blockade.

Rear Admiral George Cockburn led the British fleet. In April 1813, he ordered the fleet to sail up the Chesapeake Bay to attack towns along the Bay and rivers. Many towns were bombarded and burned and many things were taken. The British particularly wanted cattle and would pay the owners for them as long as the owner did not resist.

In response to this, a lookout was established at Point Lookout in **St. Mary's County** to report the number of British ships, the number of cannons on board, and any other helpful information that could be observed. These reports were relayed to Washington, Annapolis, and Baltimore as quickly as possible.

It was a terrible time for the people living along the Bay and rivers. The British took over St. Clement's, St. Catherine, and St. George Islands and completely destroyed everything on them. Eventually they proceeded up the Potomac River and burned part of Washington. They attempted to burn Baltimore, but they were unsuccessful.

Leonard Town in St. Mary's County was occupied by Admiral Cockburn's troops for a time. They destroyed some buildings in and near town but did not damage the courthouse. Two women, Mrs. Thomson and Eliza Key, saved it by telling the British that the courthouse was also used as a place of worship, so the British spared the building.

Eliza Key was a cousin of Francis Scott Key who wrote the "Star-Spangled Banner" during the Battle of Baltimore.   *FUN FACT*

Throughout the summer of 1814, the citizens of **Calvert County** also had the challenge of defending themselves against the British. Soldiers were stationed along the Patuxent River to protect the citizens and the county from the British. After Admiral Sir George Cockburn assumed command of the British forces, raids along the river and Bay increased. Commodore Joshua Barney and his men attempted to defend the river with cannons on barges. The British had rockets that could travel farther than the Americans' cannons, so Barney and his men retreated into St. Leonard's Creek. The fighting continued, and the Americans set up cannons on shore as well. On June 10, the British retreated because of damage to their ships, but they continued to blockade the creek. Near the end of June, Barney successfully launched a surprise dawn attack against the British. The Chesapeake flotilla managed to escape the creek and moved farther up the Patuxent.

During the time of this conflict, the British sent raiding parties ashore. They burned some plantation homes and robbed the owners. They also destroyed many towns.

On July 18, 1814, a surprise attack occurred at Huntingtown, and the entire town was burned to the ground. Then the British burned the courthouse and some other buildings at Prince Frederick. Fortunately, records stored in the courthouse were saved. Much of the tobacco crop was destroyed as were some warehouses where tobacco was stored. The Calvert County Militia drove the British off from Prince Frederick so their ships retreated down the Patuxent to await reinforcements.

In mid-August, British reinforcements arrived. Transport ships took troops up the river. After landing at the town of Benedict, the troops marched to Washington. On their way, they destroyed many towns and plantations. The Americans tried to repel the invasion, but they were defeated by the British at the Battle of Bladensburg. The British went on to Washington. They occupied the city and eventually burned the White House and other important buildings. The British found Commodore Barney's ships in a narrow section of the Patuxent River near Upper Marlboro in Prince George's County. To prevent the British from capturing his ships, Commodore Barney ordered them to be sunk, so the ships were blown up. Some of the wreckage has been discovered in the river.

Several men from Calvert County distinguished themselves in the war. These include General James Wilkinson who led the last invasion of Canada during the war. He had earlier captured the city of Mobile, Alabama, from the British. Colonel William Lawrence from Islington (the family plantation in Calvert County) was given command of the defenses of Mobile after General Wilkinson left. When the British attacked to retake the town, Colonel Lawrence and his troops defeated them. This was a major defeat for the British.

The British sailed near the town of Port Tobacco in **Charles County** at least two times during the war. No major battles were fought in the county, though many of its citizens fought against the British in other areas.

It took only 130 American soldiers to defeat 1,300 British at the Battle of Mobile. *FUN FACT*

The Treaty of Ghent was signed December 24, 1814, ending the war. The news did not reach America immediately. The treaty was not ratified until February 17, 1815. During this time the British continued to raid St. Mary's County, kidnapping slaves and destroying boats. It was reported to Governor Levin Winder that all British ships finally left the area on January 14 and 15, 1815.

SLAVERY, THE CIVIL WAR, AND EVENTS THAT FOLLOWED

Slavery

Slavery was a fact of life in southern Maryland before the Civil War. Many tobacco plantation owners had more than fifty slaves who worked at a variety of jobs, but mainly in the tobacco fields. Indentured servants were used at first, but they worked only four or five years until they could buy their own farms. The success of a tobacco plantation depended on having enough help to harvest a crop. Plantation owners turned to slavery as a source of workers. At first, slaves were brought from the West Indies. After 1695, most of them came directly from Africa.

The Royal Africa Company of England brought slaves to this country. Slave trading was one of the biggest businesses in the world during the 1700s. In southern Maryland, there were slave-selling stations in Benedict and Nottingham. Adult slaves captured in Africa had knowledge of farming, irrigation, weaving, and other skills needed in the colony. And they brought a wealth of stories, songs, dances, and cultural experiences that would enrich the new country.

Many owners treated their slaves well and took care of them. If they did not, no one interfered, since this was considered a private matter.

Underground Railroad

Slaves attempting to escape to freedom often traveled through Maryland along a route known as the Underground Railroad. This was a series of homes, farms, and churches—called stations—which were owned by people who were against slavery. The slaves were allowed to stay at these stations as they traveled north. There is little evidence of Underground Railroad activity in the southern Maryland region except for a tunnel under St. Ignatius Churchyard in Port Tobacco. Most of the slaves traveled through Montgomery, Howard, and other counties on their way to freedom.

The Civil War

The Civil War was fought for many reasons, including slavery and states' rights. Maryland officially supported the Union even though it was a slave-holding state, because Thomas Hicks, Maryland's governor in 1861, believed the states should remain as one country.

The Civil War lasted from April 12, 1861, to April 9, 1865. For those four years, **St. Mary's County** did not follow Maryland's official position of siding with the Union cause. Most people in the county were pro-South and proud of it. St. Mary's County had a plantation economy that was much more like the southern United States than the industrial North. Although many people in southern Maryland knew slavery was wrong, they depended on the slaves for economic reasons, and they fought for the way of life that slavery provided.

Before the war started, people from St. Mary's began to form rifle companies such as the St. Mary's Dragoons and Riley's Rifles. More men joined the Confederate Army after the war started. Women sewed Confederate flags, and everyone read the *St. Mary's Beacon,* the pro-South county newspaper, for news.

The Union Army was aware that the county had chosen to support the South, so they occupied the county to stay in control. People known to be actively working for the South were arrested. The *St. Mary's Beacon* ran editorials protesting Union tactics. In April 1863, Union officials arrested the editor, J. S. Downs, and shut down the newspaper for five months.

The Union Army blockaded the Patuxent River, but people tried to cross anyway. Men such as John Bradburn, James Foxwell, and Wesley Thomas smuggled supplies, food, and clothing to the Confederate Army. These men were caught, but Bradburn escaped and returned to smuggling.

Most people think of the Civil War as being fought mainly by white men, but many black men also fought. Naturally, most fought on the side of the Union. In October 1862, a recruitment center for black men was set up in Charles County. The white plantation owners did not want their slaves to fight, even though the U.S. government promised to pay them $300 for each slave who signed up. Soon there were enough recruits to organize the Ninth Regiment Infantry Colored Troops. Two others were formed soon afterward—the nineteenth and the thirtieth. Some black men joined the Army of the Potomac. All in all, 588 black soldiers from St. Mary's County fought for the Union; of those,125 died.

One of the most famous men from St. Mary's County to fight on the Confederate side was Colonel Richard Thomas, also known as Zarvona. His daring plan to capture a Union steamboat would probably be made into a movie if it happened today. He went to Baltimore and found twelve men to help him with his plan. He disguised himself as a French lady, and his helpers disguised themselves as migrant workers on their way to the fields. They booked passage on the steamboat *St. Nicholas.* In their baggage they carried guns and other weapons. When the steamboat was well on her way, the weapons were pulled out and the steamboat was captured. Several other Union cargo ships were also captured but not the ship Zarvona most wanted. He planned to capture a Union warship called *Pawnee,* but its commander had been killed and it had turned back to Washington. Later, on his way to New York for more weapons, Zarvona was arrested and imprisoned. His imprisonment affected his health, and he died in 1875.

Another man from St. Mary's County fought the war from his position in Congress. Benjamin Gwinn Harris served in the thirty-eighth and thirty-ninth Congress as a representative of the fifth district. Daily, he made speeches against waging war against southern states, interfering in elections, and freeing slaves without paying owners for them. Finally, he was arrested for treason, but his arrest occurred after the war had ended, and President Johnson eventually pardoned him.

The Union Army set up four facilities in St. Mary's County to take advantage of its strategic location on the Bay. This helped them maintain control of the county. There was a coaling station on St. Indigoes Creek, a supply depot at Bushwood Wharf, and a hospital and a prison camp at Point Lookout.

William Allen offered the Union Army land and buildings at Point Lookout. These were to be used for a military hospital. The buildings had been a hotel complex, but due to the war, no tourists were coming. The U.S. government added other buildings. Sixteen buildings were constructed in a circle like the spokes of a wheel. The hospital was named Hammond Hospital after W.A. Hammond, surgeon general of the United States. Less than a year later, the government decided to establish a prison camp there. Conditions at the camp, like at most prison camps in the Civil War, were awful. There was no building to house the prisoners so they lived in tents. Everything was dirty, and there was not enough food or water. Many men died there in the heat of summer and cold of winter. The hospital and prison camp were used from the time of their construction until the end of the war. There is now a monument at Point Lookout to the Confederate soldiers who died there. The bronze plaques list 3,389 names.

Calvert County entered the war allied with the South. Men from the county joined the Confederate Army. The Union Army was aware of this, so troops occupied Calvert as they did in St. Mary's. They set up camp on Battle Creek and built an arsenal and a prison for Confederate soldiers.

Residents of Calvert County set up a smuggling organization across the Patuxent River at Brooke Place Manor to smuggle medicine and other supplies to the Confederate Army in Virginia. Under cover of darkness, they tried to sneak by Union ships stationed in the Chesapeake Bay.

In 1863, the Emancipation Proclamation was issued freeing the slaves in the South. Many of the slaves who worked on tobacco plantations refused to work. Although the proclamation did not actually include Maryland, the slaves there wanted to be free like the slaves in the South. There were about 4,600 slaves in Calvert County at the time. Some of them returned to work for pay, but most plantations went out of business due to lack of help.

In **Charles County** on December 18, 1860, a meeting was held to discuss a plan of action for the coming war and the presidential election. Resolutions were written to censure (punish) anyone who voted for Lincoln.

There was only one volunteer for the Union Army from Charles County. By the time of the draft for soldiers, most of the young men had already gone to Virginia to join the Confederate Army of the South.

Charles County saw some action during the Civil War, though no large battles were fought there. Confederate blockade-runners used Port Tobacco as a center of operations. (Blockade-runners were the people and ships that were able to move past the Union's blockade of the Bay.) Men worked in secrecy, smuggling people, food, mail, supplies, and communications. Port Tobacco was an important link in the southern spy network that existed from the South all the way to Canada.

Charles County was occupied by Union troops who considered the county to be enemy territory since its people were sympathetic to the South. There were armed soldiers patrolling throughout the county. Colonel Charles Graham stationed his troops at Port Tobacco in the courthouse. Other Union troops eventually came, including General Daniel Sickles's Excelsior Brigade from New York. One patrol was stationed near Major Watson's house, but he bragged later that Confederate mail that came to him was sent on and "not one [Confederate] letter entrusted to me was ever lost." Dr. Snowden Dent was another important link in the Confederate mail route.

Olivia Floyd was a spy for the Confederacy during the Civil War. She was known as Miss Olivia, and she lived at Rose Hill. She relayed messages from as far away as Canada to the southern armies in Virginia.

Rose O'Neal Greenhow also acted as a secret agent for the Confederates in Charles County although she was originally from Montgomery County. Her nickname was Wild Rose. She is one of the most

One night Miss Olivia hid a message in the andirons at the fireplace. When the Union soldiers searched her house, they rested their feet on the andirons but did not find the message.

famous spies of the Civil War. One of her secret messages to General Pierre G.T. Beauregard helped him win the Battle of Bull Run. Her spying helped the Confederacy win the Battle of Manassas.

Rose Greenhow wrote her memoirs and received her royalties (payment) in gold. On her return trip from London where the memoirs were sold, she attempted to avoid Union gunboats by going to shore in a rowboat. She never made it to shore because the boat capsized and the weight of the gold dragged her down.

In 1862, steamboats stopped hauling passengers because the U.S. government seized them to transport troops and supplies. Three of these steamboats were *Freeborn, Resolute,* and *Baltimore.* The Bay and rivers were blockaded. Union gunboats patrolled the Potomac River and Pope's Creek.

On November 10, 1861, a large balloon developed by Thaddeus Lowe, lifted off from Mattawoman Creek. It was used to spy on Confederate batteries and troop positions in Virginia. This was the first time any aircraft had been used for military purposes.

Many interesting expressions used today were used during the Civil War: hunky-dory, greenhorn, skedaddle, fit as a fiddle, fit to be tied, jailbird, hard knocks, and played out. Others not so familiar were sawbones (a surgeon), bread basket (stomach), Bully! (Hurrah! or Yeah!), possum (a buddy or pal), goobers (peanuts). There were many names for liquor, including joy juice, tar water, nokum stiff, bark juice, and 'shine.

After the War

The years following the Civil War were as difficult for southern Maryland as they were for states in the Deep South. The war ended the

In the late 1800s, southern Maryland became a popular resort. People enjoyed visits to the beaches in the summer. Chesapeake Beach and Piney Point were especially popular.

THE EARLY TWENTIETH CENTURY

In the early part of the twentieth century, there was very little change in southern Maryland. The population remained fairly constant, as did the economy. Attitudes about family life and religion remained the same. People continued to make a living by farming or by harvesting fish and shellfish from the Bay and rivers. During Prohibition in the 1920s, southern Maryland became famous for bootlegging (smuggling and selling illegal liquor). Though the depression in the 1930s caused hard times, people did not have to rely on charity to feed their families. They continued to fish and work their farms. Electricity came to the area, eliminating the need for candles to light people's homes.

In August 1933, a terrible storm hit southern Maryland. Extremely high tides flooded much of the area, destroying buildings and crops. The water was so deep that people were rescued from their homes by boats. They did not have much warning of the coming storm since weather forecasting was not a well-developed science at that time.

The military arrived in 1942 with the establishment of the Naval Air Station Patuxent River. The economy improved because many businesses opened to serve the growing population. The construction of the base brought new residents and new, higher-paying jobs.

NOT-SO-FUN FACT	There was not enough housing available for the construction workers who came to build the naval base. Some lived and slept outdoors, and others lived in tents and trailers.

In 1942, a construction camp was built to house 3,300 construction workers. Unfortunately, this camp became a high crime area with fights, stabbings, and thefts, so many people moved away.

Bus routes were extended which helped the general public as well as the workers. Highways were widened and improved. In 1943, a Pennsylvania rail line was completed to haul freight between the base and Brandywine, Maryland.

In **St. Mary's County** most people made their living either on the water, by fishing or oystering, or on the land, by farming. Much tobacco was still grown. There were also a number of grain mills around the county such as those at Great Mills. These have been restored. There was a mill on Route 5 near Leonardtown. Francis Cecil (who was called Roe Cecil) ran it. There was another one near Charlotte Hall, in addition to Yowaiski's Grain Mill.

Calvert County did not progress rapidly during the earliest part of the century. People continued to fish and grow tobacco, as they had since the county was established. Although cars and trucks were invented, Calvert County residents continued to depend on their horses and oxen for much of their transportation. The lumber industry in the county began to grow with markets in Baltimore. The timber was transported by water. Many young men left Calvert County and went to Baltimore to work in factories as the country prepared for World War I.

After World War I, there was a period of growth in Calvert County. Prince Frederick grew rapidly and a new library, a movie theater, a high school, and a courthouse were built. There were a number of roads built in the county, thus ending its isolation from other counties.

In the early 1920s, the Chesapeake Biological Laboratory was built at Solomons. Under the leadership of Dr. Reginald V. Truitt, scientists studied marine life of the Chesapeake Bay, such as clams, oysters, crabs, fish, and jellyfish, and they encouraged conservation. The laboratory is still in existence today and is funded by the state. It monitors conditions for life in the Bay.

During the twentieth century, **Charles County** grew more than at any other time in its history. Businesses and industries moved to the county and the Chamber of Commerce was formed. The schools were improved. People could heat their homes by gas or oil rather than by wood. People bought automobiles, creating a need for more and better roads to be built.

Electricity came to the counties in the late 1930s. The first power plant was built in Charles County at Pope's Creek, providing power to about six hundred customers. The cooperative that built the power plant is still in existence today. However, it no longer generates its own electricity. It buys electricity from another source.

Transportation

Steamboats were an important means of transportation during the early part of the century. They traveled up and down the Bay and rivers carrying passengers and freight. They docked at landings such as Millstone Landing on the Patuxent River, which later served as a ferry landing for ferries carrying cars between **St. Mary's County** and Solomons in Calvert County. People traveled to and from Baltimore and shipped freight such as tobacco, peaches, apples, tomatoes, and blackberries. The boats landed at the Tobacco Growers Warehouse on Light Street in Baltimore.

In 1943, a railroad line opened to serve the Naval Air Station. This freight line was extended from the Brandywine/Mechanicsville line that had been in operation since the 1880s.

After World War I, most people were still using horses and horse-drawn buggies for transportation. A new highway opened in **Calvert County** making it easier to travel. Route 2 was built from Owings in the northern part of the county to Solomons at the southern end. This was the only paved road in the county at that time. This gave people a faster way to get to Baltimore and Washington. They began to buy cars and travel in and out of the county. The next road to be hard-surfaced was Route 231, Church Street.

Route 301 runs through **Charles County.** It is the main commuter and freight route through the county and many businesses are located along it. Other main roads are Maryland Route 5 and Maryland Route 210. The Conrail train also runs through the region, and the depth of the channel in the Potomac River makes it possible to ship freight directly to Charles County.

World War I

World War I started when a Serbian nationalist named Gavrilo Princip shot Archduke Francis Ferdinand of Austria-Hungary. This murder started a war that had been brewing for some time. European countries built up large armies and formed military alliances with each other. The countries were also trying to colonize other parts of the world. Britain, France, and Russia formed the Allies and backed Serbia. Austria-Hungary and Germany opposed them and became known as the Central Powers. As the war continued, other countries took sides and joined one of these alliances.

The United States entered World War I in 1917 because the Germans sank many of its merchant ships. American troops fought with other Allied troops against Germany and the other Central Powers.

With the start of World War I, citizens of **St. Mary's County** worried about German U-boats (submarines) coming up the Bay. In 1916 men enlisted in the recently activated National Guard. After the United States entered the war on April 6, 1917, many men were drafted or enlisted in the armed services.

Some people who did not fight worked in shipbuilding. Women did their part by serving as nurses, running the Red Cross, and making "comfort" bags (filled with items needed by soldiers). There were shortages of food, fuel, and other things, so these were rationed. This meant that people were allowed only a certain amount of each item. During the war, there was an epidemic of influenza (flu) that caused many deaths. There were also casualties from the war. A memorial to veterans, dedicated in November 1921, stands in downtown Leonardtown.

When war broke out, men from **Calvert County** joined the various military services. A memorial to those who served is located on the grounds of the courthouse in Prince Frederick.

Many people who did not fight in the war went to Baltimore to work in war plants, which manufactured various armaments (weapons), equipment, and supplies needed by the armies.

Many men in **Charles County** also fought in World War I. In 1919, the American Legion was founded, and it is still active in the county today. The organization represents veterans from all wars. Members march in patriotic parades and place flags on veterans' graves. Throughout the United States, veterans gather to honor and remember their fellow troops who lost their lives in war.

World War II

World War II began in Europe in 1939 as a conflict between Germany and two countries that did not agree with Germany's policies—Britain and France. The war eventually spread to other parts of the world and involved every major power in the world.

The United States entered World War II in December 1941, in response to the Japanese attack on Pearl Harbor, Hawaii.

World War II changed **St. Mary's County** forever even though there were no battles fought there. The Naval Air Station Patuxent River was built, bringing thousands more people to the county. The economy started to grow. The draft was established in the county in 1940 and men who did not enlist were required to join the military to fight. People not in the military were encouraged to take part by becoming air raid wardens or by joining the rescue squads, auxiliary police, and medical corps.

Soldiers were brought to St. Mary's County to practice landing procedures from boats. Many of these men later were sent to the South Pacific.

A munitions plant was located in St. Mary's County and ammunition is still being found in the vicinity, preventing the area from being developed.

Calvert County became involved in the war after Germans mined the mouth of the Chesapeake Bay in 1942. Mines are small explosives placed underground or underwater and designed to destroy enemy soldiers, vehicles, and ships.

The navy bought land for a base, displacing people from their homes. In 1942 and 1943, the base was built along the lower Patuxent River near Solomons and Point Patience, where the river was deep and wide. The county's shorelines were used for training military units in amphibious warfare.

FUN FACT   At the Naval Air Station Patuxent River, men practiced landing from ships in preparation for landings in enemy territory. Areas of the Patuxent River were used by hundreds of landing barges. The men who would lead the invasion of Europe at Normandy were trained here because the coastlines are similar.

A mine testing station was established at Point Patience. The Patuxent River is very deep at this point. It was a good place to test mines and depth charges that were used to blow up enemy ships and submarines. Citizens of the area were concerned because these explosions killed large numbers of fish. Watermen were not allowed to fish when the mouth of the Patuxent River was closed for mine and torpedo testing.

All this military activity in the county, as well as the Naval Air Station Patuxent River in nearby St. Mary's County, led to great improvements in Calvert County's economy. Wages were high, military people shopped in the county, and property values went up. Shipbuilding was an important industry. Many people worked at the M. M. Davis Shipyard, building minesweepers and army transport boats.

After World War II, Calvert County continued to do well economically, as it had during the war. The new roads brought visitors into the county to see the cliffs and the beautiful views of the Chesapeake Bay. Some built homes and stayed. It became possible to live in Calvert County and commute to work in Annapolis or Washington.

World War II had a large impact on **Charles County.** Before the war, tobacco was the main crop and the Depression was ending. The British put an embargo on tobacco and farmers became concerned since Britain was still a large market for their crop. People followed the news of the war in Europe and listened for draft numbers to be drawn.

The powder plant at Indian Head, built in the 1800s, began to grow. The navy built the community of Potomac Heights to house the large number of workers who were needed there. The Indian Head Highway was completed by the U.S government in 1943. Many things were rationed as they were elsewhere in the country including rubber, sugar, and gasoline. Citizens read the newspapers looking for news of friends or relatives overseas. The growth in the county during this time was a problem because of the lack of services to support the growth. In 1949, voters elected to legalize slot machines (used to gamble for money) to provide money for some of the projects.

Other Wars

Southern Marylanders have served in other conflicts since World War II. These include the Korean War, the Vietnam War, and the Persian Gulf War.

THE LATE TWENTIETH CENTURY

Lifestyles

Before 1960, southern Maryland had a very rural, agriculture-based lifestyle. Tobacco was still an important economic product. After 1960, the lifestyle of southern Marylanders changed as new roads and bridges were built. Many people moved into the region from the cities and suburbs of Baltimore and Washington. They became commuters to and from work.

Many housing developments have been built, and tourists are encouraged to visit. People live a more modern lifestyle with numerous shopping malls and marinas for recreational boats. Many of the old traditions are falling away. Even with all this, **St. Mary's County** remains the most rural section of southern Maryland.

The Naval Air Station Patuxent River in St. Mary's County and the Naval Surface Warfare Center at Indian Head in Charles County have promoted economic and population growth in those counties. They have had the same impact in nearby Calvert County.

Hunting was always a popular sport in **Calvert County,** and after World War II, it became even more so. People came from nearby cities to hunt in the marshes, as they still do today. They hide in duck blinds, which are wooden platforms covered in rushes, reeds, and tree branches.

Sport fishing, boating, and water recreation have also grown in popularity. For many years there has been a rivalry on the Chesapeake Bay between powerboat owners and sailboat owners. Sailors feel that the powerboats pollute the environment and are noisy. One reason powerboat owners dislike the sailboats is because they must yield to the slower craft.

Sailors call powerboaters "stinkpotters" because of the exhaust from the motors. The powerboaters call the sailors "ragbaggers" because of their sails.   *FUN FACT*

In **Charles County,** recreation and occupations relate to the water. Residents enjoy boating and swimming. Watermen harvest oysters and crabs. People also use the more than 10,000 acres of parks located in the county. Golf is a popular pastime, as is bass fishing.

Citizens enjoy the Mattawoman Creek Art Center, the College of Southern Maryland's Fine Arts Center and the six state parks and eight county parks. They attend plays given by the Port Tobacco Players.

Baltimore and Washington, D.C., are close enough that people can take advantage of the museums, shows, and concerts in these cities.

Transportation

Transportation improved considerably in southern Maryland during the last half of the twentieth century as new roads were built. In 1950, a bridge was built across the Patuxent at Benedict to connect Charles County and Calvert County. In 1977, the Thomas Johnson Bridge was built across the Patuxent at Solomons connecting Calvert County to St. Mary's County.

Maryland Route 5 runs the length of St. Mary's County. Routes 2 and 4 join in the northern part of Calvert County and continue southward as one highway to Solomons. A number of secondary roads branch off from Routes 2 and 4.

The nearest airports are St. Mary's Regional Airport in St. Mary's County, Baltimore Washington International (BWI) near Baltimore, and Ronald Reagan Washington National and Washington Dulles International near Washington.

In 1940, the Governor Harry W. Nice Memorial Bridge was opened from Charles County to Virginia. This bridge actually opened Charles County to the rest of the region via Route 301. This continues to be one of the most important roads in the county. During the late 1990s, traffic along Route 301 increased and residents of the area complained to their local government. A task force was established to study the problem. Unfortunately, the study brought no solution.

Courts and Public Service Agencies

Courts

The District Court of Maryland hears cases concerning landlord and tenant disagreements and motor vehicle violations. It hears criminal cases if the sentence is less than three years in prison or the fine is less than $2,500 or both, and it hears civil cases involving fines up to $20,000. There are no juries in the district court. If a crime requires a jury trial, the case must be heard in the circuit court. The district courts for all three southern Maryland counties are part of District 4.

The District Court of Maryland for **St. Mary's County** has one judge appointed by the governor with approval of the senate for a ten-year term. District court is held in the Joseph D. Carter Building on Leonard Hall Drive in Leonardtown.

The District Court of Maryland for **Calvert County** has one judge appointed by the governor with senate approval to serve a ten-year term. Court is held on Duke Street in Prince Frederick.

The District Court of Maryland for **Charles County** has two judges appointed by the governor with senate approval to serve a ten-year term. Court is held on Charles Street in La Plata.

The Circuit Court of Maryland has judges appointed by the governor with approval from the senate. These must also get voter approval every fifteen years for continued service. This court hears criminal cases, serious civil cases, and juvenile cases. It hears condemnation cases when the government needs someone's land for highways, public buildings, parks, and so forth. It also hears appeals from the district court.

The Circuit Court of Maryland for **St. Mary's County** is part of the seventh Judicial District including Calvert, Charles, Prince George's, and St. Mary's Counties. Circuit court has three judges and is held in the Circuit Court Building on Leonard Hall Drive.

The Circuit Court of Maryland for **Calvert County** is held in the courthouse on Main Street in Prince Frederick. This court has two circuit court judges and one domestic master, a person who hears cases involving divorces and juvenile cases. The judges are elected and/or appointed for a fifteen-year term.

The Circuit Court of Maryland for **Charles County** is held in the courthouse on Charles Street in La Plata. The court has four judges appointed by the governor or elected to fifteen-year terms.

Orphans Court is also held in these counties, hearing cases concerning wills and estates. Each county has three judges who are elected to four-year terms.

Orphans Court in **St. Mary's County** is held in the Joseph D. Carter Building on Leonard Hall Drive.

Orphans Court for **Calvert County** is held in the courthouse on Main Street in Prince Frederick.

Orphans Court for **Charles County** is held in the courthouse on Charles Street in La Plata.

Law Enforcement Agencies

The office of sheriff originated in 992 A.D. in England. The word sheriff comes from "shire reeve," shire meaning "tract of land," and reeve meaning "king's man." The duties of the officer were to maintain order and collect taxes.

The first sheriffs of St. Mary's were appointed by the governor and served until the governor decided to appoint new officers. In 1692, the

assembly passed an act limiting the term of the sheriff to two years and later to three years. The position was well paid.

The sheriff's duties included issuing warrants, collecting county and provincial taxes, issuing summonses to witnesses for trials, taking custody of prisoners, and carrying out punishments. The sheriff was also responsible for holding elections.

Today the office of sheriff in **St. Mary's County** is an elected position and is a four-year term. The sheriff's department investigates crime and enforces drug and other laws. The officer takes care of security at the courthouses and at corrections facilities. Sheriffs serve summonses to court, warrants for arrest, and court orders. Their duties also include traffic safety. The St. Mary's Sheriff's Department has an underwater recovery unit and a canine unit with a drug detection dog. Officers give lectures on crime prevention.

The **Calvert County** Sheriff's Office dates back to the 1600s when the high sheriff was the main law enforcement officer. In addition, he was in charge of all elections held at the county courthouse. In those days, only landowners had the right to vote. The first sheriff was Richard Collett who was appointed to the post around 1654.

Today the sheriff's office is located in the courthouse on Main Street. There are approximately seventy-five deputies. Since there is no county police department, the sheriff's office is full service, handling law enforcement as well as court duties. The sheriff is elected to a four-year term.

The Sheriff's Office of **Charles County** is a full-service department since there is no county police department. There are five divisions in the office: patrol, corrections, criminal investigations, technical services, and special services. The sheriff's office employs about three hundred people. Offices are located at La Plata, Indian Head, and Waldorf.

The Maryland State Police are involved in crime investigation, traffic and motor vehicle law enforcement, and drugs and weapons investigations. They respond to calls concerning vandalism, domestic violence, murder, robbery, assault, and many other civil and criminal violations. Some troopers have dogs that work with them sniffing out drugs or tracking people who are lost or wanted by the police.

The troopers of the Maryland State Police serve **St. Mary's County** from their barracks in Leonardtown. They have a mobile crime unit available to them when needed, and a canine corps is assigned to them.

Since November 1970, southern Maryland has had the benefit of the state police MedEvac helicopter stationed at the St. Mary's Airport.

The state police barracks in **Calvert County** is located at the corner of Main and Duke Streets in Prince Frederick.

In **Charles County,** the state police barracks is located in La Plata on Route 301. There are thirty troopers who serve in the county. Two state police MedEvac helicopters are stationed at nearby military air bases to fly critically ill or injured people to hospitals.

Fire Departments

There are seven fire departments in **St. Mary's County,** all manned by volunteers. There are also six volunteer rescue squads. The rescue squads depend on donations, while the fire departments are funded by a fire tax.

One of the fire departments in Mechanicsville was established in 1934. It began when forty town citizens gathered on the porch of All Faith's Parish Hall to discuss ways to provide fire protection for the village.

The first fire department in **Calvert County** was at North Beach. The second department in Prince Frederick was originally known as the

Calvert County Volunteer Fire Department. It was established in the mid-1920s. It was disbanded in the early1930s due to lack of funds. It was reestablished in the fall of 1940 after several large fires in the county. Its name was changed in 1984 to Prince Frederick Volunteer Fire Department. The third fire department in the county was added to the Solomons Volunteer Rescue Squad in 1964. The towns of Huntingtown, Dunkirk, and Chesapeake Beach also have fire companies. Rescue squads also serve the county.

Charles County has volunteer fire departments in La Plata, Indian Head, Hughesville, Waldorf, Cobb Island, Benedict, Nanjemoy, Potomac Heights, Marbury, Bryans Road, and Bel Alton. Citizens of Charles County pay a fire tax to help support their fire departments. Fundraisers are held to earn additional money.

Charles County's emergency medical crews are also volunteers. The Charles County Mobile Intensive Care Unit has paramedics, cardiac rescue technicians, and emergency medical technicians—all members of ambulance and emergency response teams. There are also eleven volunteer rescue squads in the county. Eight are associated with fire departments and three are independent.

ST. MARY'S COUNTY (1637)

The Maryland colony began in 1634 with the settlement of the area that would later become St. Mary's County. Named after the Virgin Mary, St. Mary's has also been called "the mother county of Maryland" and "the birthplace of religious freedom." It is the southernmost county on the western shore of the Chesapeake Bay.

According to the 1990 census, there were 75,974 people living in the county. In 1995, the population was almost 81,000. By 2010, it is predicted to be 92,500.

Establishment of the County

St. Mary's was the first county established in Maryland. When the colonists arrived, the St. Mary's settlement was considered to be the province of Maryland. Thirty square miles of land were bought from the Indians. The first references to St. Mary's as a county are found in records from 1637.

County Seat

The first county seat of St. Mary's County was St. Maries City, Maryland's oldest town. In 1635, the Maryland General Assembly met there at the homes of Governor Leonard Calvert and Secretary John Lewger. In the 1660s, the Assembly bought a home in St. Mary's City called Governor's Field, which had belonged to the colony's first two governors. Half of it was used as a seat of government and the other half was rented to a man who ran it as an inn, called an ordinary. One state house was built in St. Mary's City in 1666, and ten years later, another was built. The second building was eventually demolished and the bricks were used to build a church. A reproduction of the brick state house stands on the site today.

In 1707, a petition from the House of Delegates was given to the assembly asking for a town to be established at Bretton Bay. Leonard Town was established on this land that was known as Shepherd's Old Fields, and it became the county seat in 1708. At first it was named Seymour Town after Governor John Seymour. Then in 1728, the General Assembly changed the name to Leonard Town after Governor Benedict Leonard Calvert, the fourth Lord Baltimore. In 1868, the two words were combined to become Leonardtown.

Before a courthouse was built, court was held near the town at the home of Thomas Cooper. The first courthouse was wooden and did not last long. A brick courthouse was built in 1736, but a fire destroyed it in March 1831. Unfortunately, many county records were lost in the fire.

Leonard Town did not have a jail for some time after its establishment. There were not many prisoners, and they were tried quickly, usually within a day or so. Most trials resulted from cases of assault and battery. If convicted, the person was charged $2 and court costs. The first jail was built in 1737. It was replaced in 1858 by a building that became known as the Old Jail. This building now houses the St. Mary's County Historical Society.

Growth in the Twentieth Century

Between 1790 and 1940, the population of St. Mary's County remained at around 15,000 residents. When construction of the Naval Air Station Patuxent River began in 1942, the population increased.

In addition to the military people stationed there, more tourists were visiting St. Mary's County. Hotels and cottages were built for people who wanted to enjoy the beaches and historic St. Mary's City.

In recent years, employment in and around the naval air station has increased significantly. The once rural land now features shopping centers and many fast-food eateries. Some residents whose roots date back to the 1600s were upset about the loss of the way of life that they had known, but they have learned to accept it. Even with these changes, St. Mary's County continues to have much open land and forests.

County Government

St. Mary's County government has a board of five county commissioners who are elected by the people living in the nine election districts in the county. They have powers conferred on them by the Maryland General Assembly. They appoint a county administrator to serve as the executive branch of the government. The commissioners have a four-year term and serve on a part-time basis. They meet weekly at the county governmental center and establish all county policies, hold public meetings, approve budgets, and perform many other duties.

Major Towns

Charlotte Hall, in the northern part of the county, began as a group of cottages built with money set aside in 1698 by the Maryland General Assembly. These cottages were erected for the care of poor people who became ill. The town was located near three springs. The Indians believed these springs, called Cool Springs, had magical healing powers. Charlotte Hall School, chartered in 1774, was built near this site. The town eventually took its name from the school. Today it has a number of homes that are more than one hundred years old.

Chaptico is located ten miles northwest of Leonardtown. It was named for the Chaptico (Choptico) Indians who once lived in the area. In 1638, it became a port on a creek of the Wicomico River. Shipping continued from Chaptico until the early 1900s when the creek filled in with silt (dirt from erosion). In 1814, the British damaged the town during the War of 1812.

Two towns with names of faraway places are **California** and **Scot-land.** California was established in 1874. It supposedly got its name from some settlers who sailed from the state of California and landed at that location. Scotland was perhaps named by a group of indentured servants who were brought to Maryland from Scotland in 1745. They named the area after their native country.

Leonardtown (formerly Leonard Town) was the first incorporated town in America. This means it was the first town to have a legal government separate from a county. Leonardtown was incorporated in 1858, but it has been the county seat of St. Mary's County since 1708.

Lexington Park was originally a small town named Jarboesville after the first postmaster of the town. When the Naval Air Station was built, the small town mushroomed in an unplanned way. The town grew as the naval base grew. Its citizens want to revitalize the town and give it a more planned look.

Mechanicsville was established about 1850. It grew around the crossroads of Old Three Notch Road and Locke Hill Road. Several stores were built at the intersection, including two millinery (hat making) shops and a blacksmith. By the 1860s, there was a sawmill, a carpentry shop, and a gristmill as well as the blacksmith. Because of these trades, the town became known as Mechanicsville.

FUN FACT   Some towns with unusual names are Hollywood, Loveville, Morganza, Helen, Budds Creek, Sandgates, Tall Timbers, St. Inigoes, Avenue, Cornfield Harbor, and Hurry.

Churches and Religion

Father Andrew White and his fellow Jesuit priests started the first Catholic parishes in Maryland. The first, at St. Mary's City, was called St. Inigoes Parish. When the colonists first landed, Father White and the other priests held services in the native longhouses and huts. About 1637, a wooden church was built at St. Mary's City.

The group also started the second parish, St. Thomas Manor, near Port Tobacco in Charles County. The church in this parish, St. Ignatius, is the oldest continuously active Catholic church in America. A third religious community was started at Newtown Manor.

St. George's Episcopal Church houses one of the oldest Anglican congregations in Maryland. It is also known as Poplar Hill and is the fourth church of this congregation. The first three were torn down or burned.

Christ Church at Chaptico was built in 1737. It was heavily damaged during the War of 1812 when British troops used it as a barn to house their horses, but it has since been repaired. A steeple was added in 1913. The church is located on Route 238 south of Chaptico.

There are also a number of black churches in the county. One of the most historic is the Ebenezer African Methodist Episcopal Church at New Market, which was built around the time of the Civil War.

NOT-SO-FUN FACT

During the War of 1812, Christ Church was used as a stable by British troops. Thinking there might be valuables hidden in the cemetery, the troops dug up many graves.

A community of Amish people moved to the area from Pennsylvania in the 1940s and 1950s. They have been successful in farming land formerly used for growing tobacco.

Today there are many congregations of worshipers in the county, such as Apostolic, Baptist, Assemblies of God, Christian Science, Church of Latter-Day Saints, Presbyterian, Seventh-Day Adventists, and others.

Education and Schools

The earliest schools in the region were run by the Jesuit priests. One was opened at Newtown Manor. Eventually, a law was passed prohibiting Catholics from operating schools. Wealthier Protestant families sent their sons to schools in Europe, and the Catholics sent their daughters as well. The girls went to convent schools. A number of schools were started by wealthy planters for the children of the area. Sometimes several families would start a school together. They thought education was very important. As the colony grew, parents wanted better local schools for their children.

In 1694, the assembly at St. Mary's City voted to tax the liquor that was imported into the colony and use the money to open public schools. Some schools did start, but there was no board of education to oversee them. In 1723, the assembly passed legislation specifically to establish one school in each county. This legislation provided for a school board of seven people called "visitors" for each school. Each schoolmaster would receive an annual salary of twenty pounds as well as a farm where he could grow food.

In 1728, another law was passed to raise money for the St. Mary's Free School. In addition every schoolmaster was required to teach a certain number of poor children as well as rich ones. The free school existed until 1774, when it and two others in Charles and Prince George's Counties were sold. The money was used to build Charlotte Hall School.

FUN FACT   Though schools were called free schools, they were not free of charge. Parents paid for their children to attend. In this case, the word free meant the schools were open to all white children whose parents could afford to send them.

In 1825, the county was divided into school districts, each with three trustees, a clerk, and a school-tax collector. Regulations were established to collect money and run the schools, but they weren't very successful. So a new law was passed to define requirements more specifically, such as school inspection, length of the school year, and what time of year to collect school taxes. This law did improve the school system.

FUN FACT   A law passed in 1825 said that schools had to be open at least six months of the year. Today's children would love to go to school only six months instead of nine or ten!

A board of school commissioners was established in 1853. These representatives of each election district met four times a year to appoint trustees, oversee school district boundary lines, and keep the financial accounts. They also evaluated teachers and renewed teaching certificates. Although the commissioners oversaw the "free schools" of the county, the schools were not really free. Everyone except the very poorest paid school taxes until 1865 when the state legislature passed a law providing for a system of education that was free for everyone in the state.

The county's school system continued to grow. In 1928, Lettie Marshall Dent became superintendent of schools for the county. During her term (between 1928 and 1957), the county and the school system changed. The many one-room schoolhouses were replaced by consolidated schools with more rooms to accommodate more pupils. High schools were built and students began to ride school buses. In 1934, a high school for black children, Banneker High School, was built in Loveville. It also held classes for elementary school students.

The first graduation from Banneker High School was in 1937. There were two students in the class. **FUN FACT**

In 1954, the U.S. Supreme Court ruled on a landmark case regarding education. In the case of *Brown vs. Board of Education of Topeka, Kansas,* the court said it was unconstitutional to have separate schools for white children and black children. (Most schools for black children in the United States were not equal to those for whites.)

In 1955, the board of education and the county commissioners appointed a committee to work on desegregation—ending the practice of sending black children to separate schools.

During 1957 and 1958, desegregation was voluntary in elementary schools. In 1959, voluntary desegregation was extended through ninth grade. Desegregation was completed by the 1967–68 school year when a new system of school zones was established for all students.

Since that time, additional schools have been built for the children of St. Mary's County. One of these is the St. Mary's Technical Center in Leonardtown, which trains students for carpentry, auto mechanics and body work, graphic arts, welding, and many other occupational skills.

There are also several fine private schools in the county including St. Mary's Ryken High School and Leonard Hall Junior Naval Academy.

The colleges in the area provide a variety of educational opportunities. St. Mary's College of Maryland is a four-year liberal arts college offering a bachelor of arts degree. The Community College at St. Mary's County is operated by the College of Southern Maryland. Students can earn a technical certificate or a two-year associate of arts degree. The Seafarers Harry Lundeberg School of Seamanship is located in Piney Point. Students study for an associate of arts degree in nautical science technology and in marine engineering technology. The Embry Riddle Aeronautical University is located at the Naval Air Station Patuxent River and offers associate's and bachelor's degrees in aeronautics.

Businesses, Industries, and Agriculture

St. Mary's County has few industries. Its major employer is the Naval Air Station.

The county is mainly agricultural, growing tobacco, soybeans, and grains as well as raising livestock. Watermen fish and oyster in the waters off St. Mary's County.

In the past, boatbuilding was an industry in the county. There is little or no boatbuilding activity today, although there are marinas for docking, storage, and boat repairs.

Many new businesses have arrived in the county in recent years, including Lowe's, Kmart, Wal-Mart, Applebee's, 7-Eleven, McDonald's, Taco Bell, NAPA Auto Parts, International House of Pancakes, and Ledo Pizza.

Fascinating Folks (Past and Present)

Father Andrew White was a Jesuit priest who came to Maryland with the first settlers aboard *Ark*. He kept a journal of the trip and the events that followed during the settlement. He offered mass when the colonists landed at St. George's Island. He and Governor Leonard Calvert erected a cross at the site. His first "chapel" was a native hut. Later, he and his fellow Jesuits started the first three Catholic parishes in Maryland. Father White worked with the natives of the area as well, trying to convert them to Christianity. In 1640, he baptized tayak Kittamaquund (Chitamachen), his wife, and their daughter. He learned the Indian language. In 1641, he moved the mission from Piscataway to Port Tobacco because the Susquehannock tribe had become a threat. He continued his work with the natives of the area. In 1645, the Puritans, who had no tolerance for other religions, arrested Father White, along with another priest, Father Thomas Copley. Both were sent back to England. Father White was sixty-five years old by then, and he did not return to Maryland.

Margaret Brent (about 1600–1671) was the first woman landowner in Maryland. She also became the first woman lawyer in America and was the first woman to request the right to vote in Maryland.

The first woman lawyer in America was known as Mistress Margaret Brent, Gentleman. This was the title given lawyers at that time.   *FUN FACT*

She was born in England and moved to America hoping to lead a less restricted life. English women were not allowed to have a profession or to go to college. Brent was well educated, though she did not go to college. She came to Maryland around 1638 with her sister, Mary, and two brothers, Giles and Fulke. Leonard Calvert granted her seventy acres of land at St. Mary's City. She added to her land by paying passage for other people to come to Maryland (she was granted a certain amount of land for each person). She took an active part in the politics of the time, even organizing troops to put down a rebellion by William Claiborne over Kent Island. Calvert knew Brent and trusted her. Just before he died, he appointed her to take care of his will and personal affairs.

Margaret Brent got into trouble after Leonard Calvert's death because Calvert had not left enough money to pay the troops hired to put down the Claiborne rebellion. Those troops were ready to hold their own revolt if they were not paid. Brent sold some cattle belonging to Cecil Calvert to pay the troops. However, she did not ask Cecil Calvert first, and he was very angry when he heard about it. The Maryland Assembly backed her and even appointed her as Cecil Calvert's lawyer.

She was responsible for managing his property and collecting any rents due. In 1648, she requested a seat in the General Assembly and the right to vote. She said she should have two votes, one as a landowner and one as lawyer for Lord Baltimore. She was turned down because the rules about women holding political office and voting were just as strict here as they were in Britain. Margaret Brent was so disgusted, she left Maryland and moved to Virginia. Because of her struggles, she is known as "America's first feminist" and "the first suffragette" (a woman who tries to get the right to vote).

Giles Brent, brother of Margaret Brent, came to Maryland in 1638. He built a house called the White House at St. Mary's City and became a leader in the colony. He was a councilman, captain of the militia, commander of Kent Island, a justice, commissioner for the treasury, and deputy governor. He married Kittamaquund's daughter Mary.

Kittamaquund (also known as Chitamachen) became emperor (tayak) of the Piscataways after murdering his older brother, Wannis, who was the tayak. He had several wives. In 1640, Father Andrew White converted him to Christianity. Kittamaquund then repented the murder of his brother and gave up all but one of his wives. Father White baptized the tayak and his wife and then married them by a Christian service. Kittamaquund changed his name to Charles and his wife changed hers to Mary. Their young daughter was also called Mary. Governor Leonard Calvert and other colony leaders attended the baptism.

Princess Mary was the daughter of Kittamaquund, tayak of the Piscataways. After being baptized at the age of seven with her parents, she went to live with and be educated by Margaret Brent. She married Margaret Brent's brother Giles Brent. Mary was known as "Princess Mary of Maryland."

William Nuthead was the first person to start a printing business south of Massachusetts. He established his business in Jamestown, Virginia, around 1682. He did not have a license, so the governor and council of Virginia told him that he could no longer run his printing business there. So he moved to St. Mary's County, where he printed documents for the colonial government.

Dinah Nuthead became the first female printer in the colony after her husband William Nuthead died. Eventually, Mrs. Nuthead moved the business to the capital, Annapolis.

Rev. Thomas Bray came to Maryland from England in 1700 and established thirty libraries in the colony. He raised money in England to buy books, and he helped to find ministers for churches in the colony.

Christopher Rousby, who also owned property in Calvert County, was collector general for the king of England in the 1680s. He collected taxes, tithes, and rents for the king. During a fight on board the ship *Quaker Ketch,* Colonel George Talbot, who was surgeon general and member of the council, stabbed him. Rousby died and was buried on the Susquehanna Plantation.

Francis M. Jarboe was the first publisher of the *St. Mary's Beacon* weekly newspaper. He was also the editor. The paper began in 1839 and was originally called the *Leonard Town Herald.* It was under the second editor, George Haydn, that the paper's name was changed.

Moll Dyer lived about a century ago near Route 5 south of Leonardtown. She was thought to be a witch. Legend has it that one freezing winter night, people of the neighborhood burned her house. She ran into the woods and then froze to death crouched beside a rock. Several days later, when she was found, imprints of her knees and hands were seen imbedded in the rock, and they are there to this day. The neighborhood residents suspect that she probably put a curse upon the people who burned her house. The stream near the site of her house is now called Moll Dyer's Run.

Dashiell Hammett is the author of the famous novel *The Thin Man,* which was made into a movie.

Ben Bradley is a former editor of the *Washington Post* newspaper. He owns Porto Bello, an old plantation in the county that was built in 1740. He became well known when his paper reported the Watergate scandal that resulted in the resignation of President Richard Nixon.

Ted Koppel, national news anchor, owns Cross Manor, an eighteenth-century estate in the county.

NOT-SO-FUN FACT   There is a legend relating to Cross Manor and the sinking of the steamship *Express* in 1878. Captain Randolph Jones and some friends were sitting in the house waiting for the return of his wife, who was a passenger on the steamship. They heard a knocking at the door, and they saw Mrs. Jones looking in the window motioning Captain Jones to open the door. But when he went to the door, no one was there. They later learned *Express* had sunk, and Mrs. Jones had died.

Natural Resources

Many of St. Mary's County's natural resources come from the Chesapeake Bay and from the Potomac and Patuxent Rivers, which run through the county. Clams, oysters, crabs, and fish are caught and marketed throughout Maryland and the United States. The Bay and rivers are a source of recreation for fishing, boating, and swimming. The county's trees are logged and used for lumber, pulpwood, and other wood products.

St. Mary's soil is mostly sand, clay, and gravel. These materials are mined and used in the construction business to make bricks and to construct driveways and roads.

Places of Interest

Historic St. Mary's City is the site of Maryland's first capital. After going to the Visitor's Center, tourists can walk to a reconstruction of the State House and a native longhouse. Signs tell where other buildings in early St. Mary's City were located. Archaeological digs are conducted at the site. Nearby is the Godiah Spray Tobacco Plantation with tour guides in colonial costume. Visitors can board a full-sized reproduction of *Dove,* the ship that brought the colonists' supplies to the New World. People can participate in walking tours, watch a video about the settlement, and browse in the gift shop at the Visitor's Center. School tours are offered. There are many special events such as Maryland Day in March, Tidewater Archaeology Weekend in July, Grand Militia Muster in October, and Giving Thanks: Hearth and Home in Colonial Maryland in November.

St. Clement's Island State Park is located on the island where Lord Baltimore's colonists first set foot on Maryland soil on March 25, 1634. At that time, the island covered about 400 acres. Having eroded over the years, the island is now about 40 acres. Visitors must go there by boat. A large cross was erected on the island in 1934 as part of Maryland's three hundredth anniversary celebration—the cross represents the one placed there in 1634 by the original settlers. The island is a state park and offers hunting, hiking, fishing, and picnicking.

The **St. Clement's Island–Potomac River Museum** commemorates the Maryland colonists' landing on St. Clement's Island with exhibits showing life in Maryland from its founding to the present. It is on the mainland across the river from St. Clement's Island. Also part of the museum are the Piney Point Lighthouse and the submerged German submarine *Black Panther.*

The **Piney Point Lighthouse** was named for the number of pine trees in the area. It is only 35 feet tall and was built for $5,000. It was the first permanent lighthouse built on the Potomac River and was manned by lighthouse keepers from 1836 to 1964 when it was deactivated. It is now a national historic site.

During the Civil War, Confederate sympathizers smuggled war supplies across Piney Point Creek from Maryland to Virginia. They often harassed and threatened the lighthouse keeper because he was a Union sympathizer.

Because several U.S. presidents vacationed at Piney Point, the lighthouse is sometimes referred to as "lighthouse of the presidents."   *FUN FACT*

Sotterley, near the town of Hollywood, is a tobacco plantation that is open to visitors interested in seeing life as it existed on similar plantations in the past. Built by James Bowles in 1717, it was called Resurrection Manor. A port of entry with its own customhouse was established on the plantation. Through marriage, the plantation came into the family of the sixth governor of Maryland, George Plater. The family enlarged the house and renamed the plantation after their ancestral home, Sotterley, in Suffolk, England. Sotterley was a major port of entry during the 1700s. A rolling road went from the house area down to the dock. Hogsheads of tobacco were rolled down the road from the barn. Part of that road is still there. Two other families, the Briscoes and the Satterlees, have lived there since the Platers. Eventually it was inherited by Mabel Satterlee Ingalls who set up a historic trust so it could be opened to the public in 1961. At one time, Sotterley had sixty-three slaves and thirteen tenant farmers. The plantation traded with Spain, Portugal, Great Britain, France, Italy, and the Caribbean Islands, as well as countries along the Caribbean coast of South America and the African Coast of the Gulf of Guinea. Today, visitors can tour the main house and gardens and see the eleven outbuildings on the property, including a smokehouse, a schoolhouse, the tobacco barn, and a slave cabin.

The **Naval Air Station Patuxent River** was commissioned on April 1, 1943. It was built because the U.S. Navy wanted to centralize its aviation testing facilities. A little over a year after it was begun, nine thousand people were working on the construction. Its 6,800 acres are located at the mouth of the Patuxent River and the Chesapeake Bay at Cedar Point on the site of two old estates, Mattapany and Susquehanna. The house at Susquehanna was eventually moved to Dearborn, Michigan. The Mattapany house is now the quarters of the senior commander on the station. Also on the station is the well-known U.S. Naval Test Pilot School. Many astronauts who have flown or are flying to outer space are graduates of the school.

The **Patuxent River Naval Air Museum,** an official U.S. Navy museum, is located at Gate 1 at the Naval Air Station in Lexington Park. Outside are seventeen planes and helicopters and soon there may be twenty. Inside the museum are hundreds of models showing different types of aircraft, a rubber airplane, a one-man helicopter, three unmanned aerial vehicles (UAV), four actual aircraft cockpits, and a number of engines that show the history of aircraft engines. Visitors can learn how aircraft are tested and about the test pilots who fly them. A gift shop sells lots of fun things.

The museum has the cupola of the **Cedar Point Lighthouse,** built in 1896. The lighthouse was used until 1925. It was finally taken down in 1981 and the cupola was given to the museum.

The **Old Town Jail** on the grounds of the courthouse in Leonardtown dates back to about 1876. The jailer lived on the first floor and upstairs were three jail cells—one for white men, one for black men, and one for women. A new jail was built during the 1950s, and the Old Jail became the St. Mary's County Historical Society Museum, which is now open to the public.

Charlotte Hall School (in the town of Charlotte Hall) was a free school for children of St. Mary's, Charles, and Prince George's Counties. It was chartered in 1774 but did not open until after the Revolutionary War. Sometime before 1850, it became a military school. When the school closed in 1976, the state bought the buildings and converted them to a veterans' hospital. Most of the buildings have been torn down but the White House remains. It was a classroom building of the school and the home of the headmaster. St. John's Episcopal Church, known as Dent's Chapel (after Reverend Hatch Dent who was the first military school principal), is on the grounds of the former school. It was built in 1883 and is listed on the National Register of Historic Places.

Point Lookout Light is located at Point Lookout, the southernmost tip of St. Mary's County. The light has been there since 1830, but its height kept it from being very important to navigation. The original house had a lantern on top, but it was only 24 feet off the ground. Eventually, the house was enlarged and the light was raised to over 40 feet. In 1966, the Coast Guard deactivated the light, and a new one was put on a nearby tower.

Tudor Hall in Leonardtown was the home of Francis Scott Key's uncle Philip Barton Key. He bought it around 1815 from the Barnes family who built the first section around 1742. Philip Key was George Washington's friend, and Washington often visited the house. It is now the research center for the Historical Society of St. Mary's County.

The site of the **Seafarers Harry Lundeberg School of Seamanship,** located on Route 249, was originally a navy torpedo station. The school of seamanship was established in 1953 as a merchant marine school and moved to this site in 1968. Harry Lundeberg was the first president of the Seafarers International Union.

The **Farm Museum** is located at the county fairgrounds on Route 5 south of Leonardtown. It has farming artifacts from the past including a replica of an old barn. There are tools used by farmers, fishermen, coopers, and other tradesmen. Many people from the area have donated items to the museum.

Cecil's Mill is a three-story building and country store. It is located in Great Mills and now features a craft shop where local art and handicrafts are sold.

Parks and Recreational Areas

Point Lookout State Park is a large park at the southernmost tip of the county. It is also the southernmost place on Maryland's western shore. At this point, the Chesapeake Bay and the Potomac and Patuxent Rivers meet. This was the site of a Union hospital and later a prison camp built during the Civil War for Confederate soldiers. There is a Civil War Museum to visit. The Point Lookout Lighthouse is also located there.

When the park is open in the summer, visitors can camp, play miniature golf, or rent boats for fishing. People can also swim, hike, and picnic in the park. There is a long fishing pier for anglers who want to stay on shore.

The **St. Mary's River State Park** is located three miles north of Great Mills. It has 2,176 acres of land and a 250-acre lake. Visitors can enjoy fishing, boating, hiking, and picnicking.

CALVERT COUNTY (1654)

Calvert County was isolated from the rest of southern Maryland until 1950. At that time, a bridge was built across the Patuxent River on Route 231, connecting the county with Benedict in Charles County. Before that, people could only access the county by ferry.

As of 1995, Calvert County's population was 63,925. By the year 2005, it is expected to expand to 85,000.

Establishment of the County

In 1650, Lord Baltimore established a new county, originally calling it Charles County. He asked his friend Robert Brooke to be "commander" of the county.

The county kept the name Charles until October 20, 1654, when the Puritans took over government of the colony. This date is considered to be the official date of the establishment of Calvert County, even though the Puritans renamed it Patuxent County using the Piscataway name meaning "the place where tobacco grows." In 1658, when the Calverts regained possession of the colony, it was finally named Calvert County.

Calvert was Maryland's fourth county (after St. Mary's, Kent, and Anne Arundel) and was much larger than it is now. Its land area originally extended north into what is now Frederick County and included much of what is now Prince George's and parts of Anne Arundel and St. Mary's Counties. Much of this land was lost when Prince George's County was established around 1696.

County Seat

Calvert County's first county seat was built by Robert Brooke in 1652 at the direction of Governor Calvert. It was located on the north side of Battle Creek. Brooke planned the county seat which was known at first as Battle Town, and later as Calvert Town. It had a courthouse, a chapel, a jail, and a few other buildings. The county seat remained in Calvert Town until 1725. That year it was moved to Prince Frederick, a town named for Prince Frederick of England who was the son of King George II.

The original courthouse burned in 1814 when the town was destroyed by the British during the War of 1812. There was another fire in 1882 that destroyed the second courthouse. In 1915, the present courthouse was built behind the site of the first two. It was remodeled in 1948 and trees were planted on the site of the first two courthouses. The courtroom has a large mural depicting a battle at St. Leonard's Creek during the War of 1812, painted by Robert and Jane Coffin.

Growth in the Twentieth Century

After World War I, Calvert County began to change. For the first time, there was money flowing into the county, improving the economy. People began to build homes along the new roads and along the shores of the Bay.

In 1954, the county celebrated its three hundredth anniversary with events such as Natural History Day, Agricultural Day, and a historical pageant reenacting famous events of Calvert County.

Between 1954 and 1976, the main highways and secondary roads in the county were widened and improved. In 1977, the Thomas Johnson Bridge was finished across the Patuxent linking Calvert County at Solomons with St. Mary's County along Route 4. This saved residents at Solomons a 44-mile trip from one county to the other. When the bridge opened, the ferry that had been running for thirty-three years closed.

During the last half of the century, a number of historic houses in the county were restored including Delhi Plantation, Sheridan Point Farm, Patuxent Manor, Warrior's Rest, and Small Reward.

One of the most important additions to Calvert County and to Maryland during this time was the Calvert Cliffs Nuclear Power Plant. It was built during the early 1970s by the Baltimore Gas and Electric Company and began operation on May 8, 1975.

The first hospital in the county was begun in 1916 and was dedicated in 1919. It is still standing but there are plans for it to become the sheriff's office. It was established through the efforts of four doctors; three were brothers and the fourth was their brother-in-law.

In 1953, a new hospital was built to serve Calvert's growing population.

County Government

The county's government consists of five commissioners who are elected to four-year terms. At least one member must be from each of Calvert County's three election districts. The commissioners serve under the *Code of Public Laws of Calvert County*. One person acts as president, though that individual has no more authority than the other members do. There are no term limits for the commissioners.

There are eight departments of the government: planning and zoning, economics and development, administration, general services, public works, community resources, public safety, and personnel. A county administrator manages the operation of these departments.

Major Towns

Chesapeake Beach is the largest incorporated town in the county. In the late 1890s, Otto Mears, who owned a railroad construction company, built a railroad line from Washington to Chesapeake Beach. He and his investors wanted to start a summer resort. They built a boardwalk, a dance pavilion, a roller coaster, and other attractions to lure people to their resort. The railroad no longer serves Chesapeake Beach; it was discontinued in 1935. However, summer tourists still enjoy vacations at this small resort on the Bay.

The original town of **Huntingtown** was destroyed by the British during the War of 1812. The town was rebuilt about three miles from the original site.

Lower Marlboro is located on the shores of the Patuxent River. It was originally known as Cox Town. In the early days of the colony, it was a port, but the river filled with silt and was too shallow for navigation. The village is supposedly the second oldest town in Maryland. So much tobacco was grown in the Lower Marlboro area in the late 1600s that the town had its own customhouse to handle imports and exports. During the 1970s, the customhouse was restored.

North Beach was incorporated in 1910. The only other incorporated town in the county is Chesapeake Beach.

Prince Frederick has been the county seat of Calvert County since 1725. Because of two fires (in 1812 and 1882), its tree-lined streets have few old buildings. Near the county courthouse is a hospital, a state police barracks, a library, and the historical society of the county.

Solomons was known as Somervell's Island from 1740 to 1814. Originally, it was called Bourne's Island. It was owned by the Bourne family as part of their estate Eltonhead Manor. In 1865, after the Civil War, Isaac Solomon purchased the island and started an oyster cannery business there. The island was settled by people who came from the Eastern Shore to work in the cannery. Solomons has a large natural harbor, 2 miles wide and up to 150 feet deep. However, it has not been used for large ships because it is so close to the much larger port of Baltimore. Also, there are no railroad lines nearby.

From 1942 through 1945 (during World War II), the navy trained thousands of sailors and marines in the skills of amphibious landing (taking troops to shore aboard special "landing craft"). Many of the men left Solomons Island in Maryland and went to serve in the Solomon Islands in the South Pacific. Others went to Normandy in France. *FUN FACT*

At one time Solomons was a separate island. Only one bridge connected the island and the mainland. The bridge was destroyed in 1933 by a hurricane. That area is now silted in, and it is impossible to tell that Solomons was once an island. There is now a road where the bridge once was.

Some towns with unusual names are Island Creek, Mutual, Plum Point, Appeal, Wallville, and Broomes Island. *FUN FACT*

Churches and Religion

Christ Church at Port Republic is probably the oldest church in the county. It was built on land called "Prevent Danger." Though there is no written record, it is believed the church was built before 1670. Parts of the earliest parish register have been preserved and are kept in the

Hall of Records in Annapolis. In 1731, a fire destroyed Christ Church, and in 1735, it was rebuilt as a brick building. There have been many renovations since then. In 1988, workers uncovered what is believed to be the foundation of a small log structure. Researchers think this was the church building that was used from 1672 to 1731.

One of Calvert County's oldest churches is All Saints Episcopal Church, built between 1774 and 1777. There is a sundial in the churchyard that Thomas John Claggett, who was rector there during the late 1700s, presented to the church. He later became the first Episcopal bishop of Maryland.

The Smithville Methodist Church in Dunkirk was dedicated in 1840. It wasn't until 1989 that a steeple and bell were added to the church.

The first church built in Prince Frederick, St. Paul's Episcopal Church, was built in 1841 and dedicated in 1848.

At one time there were several Quaker communities in Calvert County, and some of the people owned slaves. Quakers from Pennsylvania began to urge those in southern Maryland to free their slaves under threat of excommunication (losing membership in the church). Most of the Quaker families freed their slaves. This made it impossible to maintain their plantations, so many were sold. The Quaker families then moved to Baltimore and other towns so their meetinghouses fell into ruin and eventually disappeared.

There are a number of other old chuches in the county such as Middleham Episcopal Church, St. John's United Methodist, Solomons United Methodist, St. Peter's Episcopal, and Our Lady Star of the Sea Roman Catholic Church.

Today many congregations worship in Calvert County, including Baptist, Catholic, Islamic, Methodist, Episcopal, Lutheran, Presbyterian, Unitarian Universalist, Church of Christ, Brethren, Church of Jesus Christ of Latter-Day Saints, Pentecostal, Seventh-Day Adventist, and several nondenominational congregations.

Education and Schools

Because most people lived on large plantations that were located far from each other, formal education was difficult in early Calvert

County. The earliest schools were held by family members or neighbors. Children wishing to study for a profession such as medicine or law went to school in England.

One of the earliest schools in Calvert County was the Lower Marlboro Academy in Lower Marlboro. It opened in 1700 in a private home. In 1775, land was given for the school and it was built through private funding by the townspeople. It closed during the Revolutionary War, then opened again in 1791. In 1854, it became part of the public school system. It was used until it burned in 1886.

One-room schoolhouses were built as the population grew. Boys often stayed home during good weather to help on the family farm. Classs did not go beyond seventh grade. The schools had no electricity and were heated with a woodstove. These schools were used in the county until 1922.

Today in the elementary and middle school, basic subjects are taught. In addition, there are special programs for academically talented students and for those with disabilities. In high school, in addition to basic subjects, students can take vocational and technical courses as well as foreign languages. There is also a foreign exchange program and a Navy Junior Reserve Officer Training Corps.

There are a number of fine private schools in the county including Calverton School, Cardinal Hickey Academy, Middleham and St. Peter's Episcopal Day School, Our Lady Star of the Sea, and the Tidewater School.

The College of Southern Maryland offers classes at the Community College at Calvert, located on Broomes Island Road at Port Republic. A new facility in Prince Frederick is now under construction. Students can take occupational classes, technical courses, and enrichment programs leading to an associate of arts degree.

There is also the Calvert Career Center in Prince Frederick which offers a number of courses including electronics, automotive mechanics, data processing, carpentry, and graphic arts.

Businesses, Industries, and Agriculture

Boatbuilding and fishing became important industries in Calvert County during the 1800s. By 1880, as many as five hundred fishing vessels had been built at Solomons. Two boats that were designed in Calvert County are the Chesapeake Bay bugeye and the skipjack. Rock Point was once a very important seafood center on the Potomac River, although most of the town is now gone. There were also tomato canneries in Solomons and Lower Marlboro, and Solomons had a cannery for oysters.

Today the Baltimore Gas and Electric Company is Calvert County's largest employer. The Calvert Memorial Hospital, DynCorp, the Calvert Nursing Center, Direct Mail Management, Inc., the Chesapeake Biological Laboratory, the Holiday Inn at Solomons, and Recorded Books, Inc. also employ large numbers of people. Several business and industrial parks are located in the county including the Calvert County Industrial Park, Patuxent Business Park, Calvert-Arundel Business Park, North Calvert Industrial Park, and Dunkirk Business Center.

Fascinating Folks (Past and Present)

Richard Preston, one of the leading colonists, settled in Calvert County. He was a Puritan and built a plantation called Preston on the Patuxent River. He was a member of the House of Burgesses (the lower house of representatives, which made the laws) and served as its speaker.

Richard Johns settled in the county around 1670 and became a leader of the Quakers. He was a successful merchant and bought a large amount of land in the county. Quaker meetings were held at his home, Angelica.

Roger Brooke Taney, born in Calvert County in 1777 at the family plantation Taney Place, was chief justice of the U.S. Supreme Court from 1836 to 1864. He is known as one of the best lawyers to ever serve on the Court. He started his career as a Calvert County delegate to the Maryland Assembly. Taney then practiced law in Annapolis, Frederick, and Baltimore City. In 1827, he was appointed attorney general of Maryland. In 1831, President Andrew Jackson appointed him attorney general of the United States. Taney became secretary of the treasury in 1833. He married Anne Key, the sister of Francis Scott Key.

Roger Brooke Taney administered the oath of office to eight presidents of the United States, from Martin Van Buren to Abraham Lincoln. *FUN FACT*

Chief Justice Taney ruled on the famous Dred Scott case, which stated that a black man whose ancestors were slaves was not entitled to rights as a citizen of the United States. It also stated that Congress could not abolish slavery in any territory acquired after the formation of the United States government.

Taney died near the end of the Civil War and is buried in Frederick in Frederick County.

Arthur Storer was a great scientist and astronomer who is believed to be one of the first people in the world to see the comet that was later named Halley's Comet. He was born in England and moved to Calvert County in 1678. He studied a number of comets, in addition to Halley's Comet.

When Arthur Storer was very young, he lived in the same house as Isaac Newton, who discovered gravity. They went to school together and became interested in astronomy. When Storer moved to America, he wrote to Newton sharing his discoveries. *FUN FACT*

Storer's gravesite is not known, but it may be on the grounds of his sister's property, where Calvert High School is now located. The high school's planetarium is named for Arthur Storer.

Thomas Johnson was born in 1732 at St. Leonard's Creek in Calvert County at a place called the Brewhouse, where his parents are also buried. He became the first governor of the new state of Maryland in 1777. He served as a justice of the Supreme Court of the United States, was involved in putting the new Constitution into effect, and helped to plan Washington, D.C. He is buried in Mt. Olivet Cemetery in Frederick.

Isaac Solomon moved to the lower Patuxent in the summer of 1866. He bought a parcel of land called Sandy Island which he later renamed Solomons Island. There he opened the first oyster business on the Patuxent River. He had hoped a railroad line would be built from Drum Point that would have enabled him to send his oysters to Baltimore. This railroad was never built, so Solomon sold his Maryland properties in 1875 and moved to Philadelphia, Pennsylvania.

Louisa Johnson Adams was the niece of Governor Thomas Johnson. In 1797, she became the wife of John Quincy Adams, who later became the sixth president of the United States. They had three sons.

Thomas Parran and **Augustus R. Sollers** are the only two men from Calvert County to serve in the U.S. Congress: Sollers in the 1860s and Parran in 1911.

Charles L. Marsh from Solomons invented deepwater oyster tongs sometime after 1877. Oyster tongs are used by oystermen to harvest oysters from the bottom of the Bay. These new tongs allowed them to find oysters in much deeper water than before, increasing the harvest.

James T. Marsh, Charles's brother, designed the first frame-and-plank sailing workboats called bugeyes. Before this, bugeyes were built from logs. Marsh established a boatyard in 1872.

Margaret Mackall Smith, the daughter of a Maryland planter, was born in St. Leonard. In 1810, she married General Zachary Taylor, who became the twelfth president in 1849. They had six children, two of whom died as babies. Due to her poor health, Margaret Smith was rarely seen in public.

FUN FACT	No one knows what Margaret Mackall Smith really looked like, because she is the only first lady who did not have a portrait painted.

Albert Gantt was one of the first former slaves in Calvert County to become successful. His owner gave him permission to fight with the Union Army as a soldier. He later became a very successful farmer and was a leader of the African-American people in Calvert County.

William Sampson Brooks was a pastor for several African Methodist Episcopal Churches around the United States. He traveled to many countries and learned to preach in Swedish. He wrote a book, *Footprints of a Black Man,* which describes one of his journeys. The administrative building of the Calvert County Schools, which originally was the first high school for African-Americans in the county, is named after Brooks.

Dr. Thomas Bourne Turner was born in 1902. He became the dean of the medical school of Johns Hopkins University.

Thomas Bourne Turner's parents owned and operated the Calvert Hotel. It was built on the site of another hotel that had burned in 1882. The hotel was home to traveling salesmen who were a big part of life at that time. Pothooks and Hangers Road was named because of the salesmen who sold their wares and yelled "pothooks and hangers!" It is now called Clyde Jones Road.

FUN FACT

Louis L. Goldstein was born in 1913 in Prince Frederick. His family owned the Prince Frederick Department Store, formerly known as the Goldstein General Store, where Goldstein and his brothers worked. He went to the University of Maryland and graduated with a law degree. In 1939, he was elected to the Maryland House of Delegates. During World War II, he served in the marines. In 1947, he became a member of the Maryland Senate and became its president in 1955. In 1958, he was elected comptroller of the treasury of Maryland. He held that post until his death in 1998. His clever poetry and "folksy" style were much loved by citizens of the state in spite of his being the state's collector of taxes.

Tom Clancy is one of America's most famous writers. He owns property and a home in Calvert County. The former insurance broker became internationally known when his first book, *The Hunt for Red October,* was published in 1984.

The **ghost of Cornhill** is a headless horseman who is sometimes seen around Halloween. No one knows who the man was. Cornhill is a property with an old brick home located between Plum Point and Prince Frederick.

FUN FACT	Cornhill is built on a ridge. Rainwater flows into the Bay from the front yard and into the Patuxent River from the back yard.

Natural Resources

The Patuxent River and its tributaries hold a wide variety of fish, shellfish, crabs, and other aquatic life.

FUN FACT	Sometimes historical treasures are found among natural resources. For example, many wrecks of boats and ships have been found at the bottom of the Patuxent River. One wreck found was from the War of 1812. Two are believed to be from the Revolution, and one small boat dates from the period of 1680 to 1720. Over six hundred pounds of cannonballs have been recovered. Near a swampy area called Spyglass Island, a complete gunboat flotilla and ships of a merchant fleet were found. These were sunk by Maryland's Commodore Joshua Barney to prevent their capture by the British.

Other natural resources include trees, especially bald cypress trees, as well as the county's many creeks and streams. Greensand (a rich and fertile soil used in gardening) and diatomite (a dry, powdery soil used as a pottery glaze or as an abrasive) are found near Dunkirk.

Places of Interest

Taney Place is the birthplace of Roger Brooke Taney, who was chief justice of the U.S. Supreme Court from 1836 to 1864. The house, located between Battle Creek and the Patuxent River, is privately owned and not open to the public.

Brooke Place Manor was the home of the Brooke family. They came to southern Maryland when invited by Lord Baltimore to establish a new county. Brooke Place Manor is located on the south side of Battle Creek and is not open to visitors.

The Baltimore Gas and Electric Company built the **Calvert Cliffs Nuclear Power Plant** at Kenwood Beach partially on land that was the Charlesgift estate. Construction was started in 1968, and the first section began generating electricity in 1975. The second section came on-line in 1977.

The plant has a visitor's center and museum located in an old tobacco barn. Animated exhibits about energy and dioramas about the surrounding county can be seen. Displays of fossils found at Calvert Cliffs are also on view. Computer games teach visitors about nuclear energy. Groups of visitors with reservations can tour the power plant.

The **Chesapeake Biological Laboratory** in Solomons is a center for the study of marine life in the Bay, including the effects of pollution on the Bay and its wildlife. It is owned by the University of Maryland's Center for Environmental Science.

The **Calvert Marine Museum** in Solomons was established in 1975 to showcase local history, artifacts, and fossils. Visitors can observe the preparation of fossils for display. They can see log canoes, bugeyes, skipjacks, oyster boats and clam boats, as well as models of the steamboats that were vital to transportation in southern Maryland. There are aquariums with live fish, oysters, sea horses, jellyfish, diamondback terrapins, and horseshoe crabs. The Discovery Room is a hands-on room for children and includes a sandbox for fossil hunting, puzzles, waterfowl decoys, and stuffed birds including a prehistoric

Pelagornis miocaenus (a Miocene seabird). There are also pictures of sharks and waterfowl.

A half-mile from the main grounds of the museum is the historic **J.C. Love and Sons Oyster House,** which displays the history of the region's commercial seafood industries.

On the grounds of the museum is the **Drum Point Lighthouse.** This hexagonal building is one of the few remaining "screwpile" lighthouses, structures that were built on large iron or wooden pilings shaped like screws. The pilings were screwed into the bottom of the Bay to firmly anchor the lighthouse. In the 1970s, Drum Point Lighthouse was moved inland from its original location to become a part of the museum. This lighthouse is on the National Register of Historic Places.

FUN FACT	It is said that a ghost slams doors and rings the bell in the Drum Point Lighthouse.

Docked at the museum is *Wm. B. Tennison,* one of the oldest log-built bugeyes on the Chesapeake Bay. Visitors can also see Squeak, a North American river otter.

The **Cove Point Lighthouse** near Solomons is the oldest tower lighthouse on the Chesapeake Bay. It stands on the grounds of the Cove Point Coast Guard Station at the entrance of the Patuxent River. It is over 150 years old and was built by John Donohoo of Havre de Grace. It has one of the most powerful lights on the Bay.

FUN FACT	Many years ago, a neighbor complained that the brightness of the Cove Point light prevented her from sleeping at night. The keeper hung a curtain at one of the windows of the lighthouse to keep the light from shining on the lady's house.

Rousby Hall is an old house in Solomons built by John Rousby. The British burned the original brick house in 1780. A weatherboard farmhouse was then built on that site. With weatherboard construction (also called clapboard), each board laps over the one below it, so water is easily shed. Rousby died in 1750 and is buried on the property. The house is privately owned.

Angelica is an old plantation located on the Upper Calvert Cliffs. It was the home of Leonard Strong, an early Puritan leader, and it was later the home of Richard Johns, a Quaker leader. The Smithsonian Institution conducts archaeological digs at the plantation. Workers have found an old Indian village and artifacts and also the remains of an inn that was built by early English settlers. The plantation is privately owned and not open to the public.

Port Republic School Number 7, a one-room schoolhouse, is located on the grounds of Christ Church in Port Republic. The school is over one hundred years old. It operated until 1932 when it was closed and abandoned. It was restored by the Calvert Retired Teachers Association and has been open to the public on weekends since July 24, 1977.

The **Chesapeake Beach Railway Museum** is located on Mears Avenue in Chesapeake Beach. This original 1898 railroad station was converted into a museum showing memorabilia from the Chesapeake Beach resort—including its boardwalk and amusement park—as well as exhibits on railroad and steamboat history. It is on the National Register of Historic Places.

The **Calvert County Historical Society** is located on Duke Street in Prince Frederick. A small exhibit shows antique furniture, clothing, photographs, and other items of interest.

The **Jefferson Patterson Park and Museum** is on Mackall Road in St. Leonard. Situated on a 544-acre property, the museum has a huge collection called "12,000 Years in the Chesapeake."

Humans are known to have continuously inhabited the Jefferson Patterson Park area longer than any other place in Maryland.   *FUN FACT*

Parks and Recreational Areas

The **Battle Creek Cypress Swamp Sanctuary** on Route 506 south of Prince Frederick is one of four locations in Maryland where cypress trees grow. They have grown there since the Pleistocene Epoch, which ended 11,000 years ago. This is the northernmost stand of bald cypress trees in the United States. This 100-acre swamp has been designated a National Natural Landmark. Visitors can hike on paths and boardwalks through the swamp to see the cypresses. Wildlife such as opossums, white-tailed deer, muskrats, and pileated woodpeckers can be seen. There is a beehive where visitors can observe bees making honey. There are audio-visual presentations, demonstrations, and exhibits about the swamp.

FUN FACT	The bald cypress trees in the Battle Creek Cypress Swamp Sanctuary can grow to 150 feet and live to be one thousand or more years old. Parts of the trees' roots stand above the water, and are called "knees."

South of Prince Frederick is **Flag Ponds Nature Park,** a 327-acre wildlife park designed to show how time affects nature. Visitors can hike the trails and the wetland boardwalk, or visit the beach, the fishing pier, the wildlife exhibits, and the observation platforms that overlook two ponds. Wildlife such as the pileated woodpecker, turkey, otter, fox, white-tailed deer, and muskrat can be seen. Bald eagles have also been sighted. Visitors can hunt for sharks' teeth along the beach. The park's name is taken from from the blue flag iris, which is native to the area.

Calvert Cliffs State Park, a 1,460-acre wooded park, is located fourteen miles south of Prince Frederick on Route 2/4. In addition to the cliffs where visitors can find fossils, there are nature trails, picnic areas, shelters, a playground, and places to fish.

CHARLES COUNTY (1658)

Charles County is known as the gateway to historic southern Maryland.
It is bordered on the north by Prince George's County, on the east by
Calvert County, on the west by the Potomac River, and on the south by
St. Mary's County. Its northern border is just eighteen miles south of
Washington, D.C., on the southern Maryland peninsula. Charles is
Maryland's fifth county and celebrated its three hundredth anniversary
(the tercentenary) in 1958.

According to the 1990 census, Charles County was Maryland's
third fastest growing county. In 1990, there were 101,154 people. By
2010, that number is expected to grow to 136,600.

Establishment of the County

Cecil Calvert created "old" Charles County on October 3, 1650, cover-
ing an area that consisted of the present Charles County as well as parts
of today's St. Mary's, Calvert, and Prince George's Counties. On April
13, 1658, the governor's council established what is now known as

Charles County, named in honor of Charles Calvert. Its boundaries were not clearly established until thirty-seven years later when, in 1695, the upper part of the area became Prince George's County.

County Seat

When "new" Charles County was first formed, its court was held in private homes and inns around Chandler's Town. This town was named after Job Chandler, the first settler in the area. In 1674, a wooden courthouse and jail were built at Moore's Lodge, thought to be located near present-day La Plata. This courthouse was used until 1728. When it fell into disrepair, a different site was chosen for a new courthouse to be built in Chandler's Town. The construction costs for this courthouse were paid with 122,000 pounds of tobacco. Since that would represent a lot of money, historians assume this building was made of brick.

In 1729, the name of the town was changed to Charlestown, in honor of Charles Calvert, the third Lord Baltimore. Later, in 1820, the name was changed again, this time to Port Tobacco. A second courthouse at the Port Tobacco site was completed in September 1821. Pictures of this courthouse still exist.

FUN FACT   The Port Tobacco courthouse was a circuit court and the judges held court twice a year: spring and fall. This was always a big event for the people. They came to sell cakes and pies around the courthouse grounds and to gossip.

The courthouse burned in 1892, except for one wing. Arson was suspected because the records stored inside the courthouse had been removed and survived the fire. After the fire, the remaining wing was used as a Baptist church. By the late 1800s, the Port Tobacco River had silted in, so large ships could no longer use it. The railroad had a station in La Plata, but not in Port Tobacco. The town began to die as people moved away. On June 4, 1895, a special election was held to determine whether La Plata or Chapel Point should be the new county seat. It was decided to move the county seat to La Plata, where it remains today.

Joseph C. Johnson designed the courthouse in La Plata. This red brick building was completed in 1896. A jail was built behind the courthouse.

The La Plata courthouse had a bell that was rung every day at 10 A.M. to announce the beginning of the court session. The rope hung from the belfry to the second floor landing.

FUN FACT

In time, the courthouse was enlarged. There were additions made in 1949, 1954, and 1974. In 1988, the county government offices, which had been in the courthouse, moved to the former Milton Somers Middle School building. Now both circuit and district courts are held there.

Growth in the Twentieth Century

During the second half of the twentieth century, Charles County continued to grow. Its location close to Washington and Baltimore led to growth in business and industry. Housing developments, restaurants, shopping centers, and malls line the main roads of the county. Farming is still important to the economy, with many farmers selling produce and other products at their farms. Charles Community College has become the College of Southern Maryland and encourages students from the entire area to study there.

County Government

Charles County has five elected county commissioners who serve for four years. The president, who is the only full-time commissioner, may live anywhere in the county, but all others must live in the district that they represent.

The commissioners are responsible for the county's budget. They oversee zoning and development, as well as the safety, health, and welfare of the citizens. They legislate county laws and ordinances and oversee policies and procedures. They appoint commissions, task forces, and boards to advise them.

Major Towns

Founded in 1683, **Benedict** became an important port on the Patuxent River for a time. At first it was called Benedict Leonard Town after the fourth Lord Baltimore. There was a customhouse, and tobacco was shipped from there until the early 1800s. During the War of 1812, the British landed at Benedict on their way to Washington in 1814.

Bryantown is located near Zekiah's Swamp. In its early days, it was a stop for travelers on their way to St. Mary's to the south and Benedict to the east.

Indian Head is located on the Potomac River about twenty-two miles south of Washington, D.C. It is the location of the Naval Surface Warfare Center. The navy built many of the houses there, but they are now privately owned. It was incorporated in 1920.

FUN FACT   There are several stories about how Indian Head was named. One, which has never been proven, says the town looks like an Indian's head from the air.

La Plata is the county seat of Charles County. It was originally a stop on the Baltimore and Potomac Railroad line, which was established in 1869 and went into service in 1873. The early town and the railroad station were located on land donated by the Chapman family. Their farm was given the French name Le Plateau because the land was so flat. The town's name was originally the same as the farm's but over the years, it was changed to La Plata. In 1873, the same year the railroad line opened, La Plata opened a post office, and the town began to grow. It was incorporated in 1888.

Marshall Hall is located thirteen miles northwest of La Plata on the Potomac River. It was originally the plantation of the Marshall family, close friends of George Washington. After the Civil War, the Marshall family had to sell much of their land. The mansion and a small cemetery are still there.

During the 1950s and 1960s, Marshall Hall was a popular gambling site for people from Washington.

Port Tobacco was named after an Indian village called Potobac which had been located at the site. Captain John Smith visited this village in 1608.

Port Tobacco was at one time very similar to Williamsburg, Virginia. It became an important harbor from which tobacco was shipped during the 1600s. It also was the county seat between 1650 and 1895. During the 1800s, the Port Tobacco River began to fill in and the larger oceangoing vessels could no longer get to the town easily. The railroad came to the county in 1872, but it did not go through Port Tobacco, so the town began to die. The town was incorporated in 1888, but in 1895, the county seat was moved to La Plata.

Today historic buildings such as the Catslide House, the rebuilt Port Tobacco Courthouse, and the Port Tobacco One-Room Schoolhouse are open to visitors. They were renovated and are maintained by the Society for the Restoration of Port Tobacco. The Thomas Stone National Historic Site is also there.

St. Charles is a large planned community. It was developed in 1965 and, when finished, will have five villages with fifteen residential neighborhoods. Each will have its own recreational area. The villages of Smallwood and Westlake are completed and Fairway began construction in 1995. St Charles also has businesses and industries and the St. Charles Town Center mall. The entire community is scheduled for completion in 2020 with an expected population of 80,000 people.

Waldorf was named in 1872, when the Baltimore and Potomac Railroad built a station at the site. Tobacco and farm products were shipped from Waldorf. People settled there in the 1700s, but the railroad brought about its growth and development.

Waldorf is located along Routes 301and 5. The town encourages businesses to locate there.

Churches and Religion

Charles County has some of the oldest churches in America. St. Ignatius Church near Port Tobacco was built in 1798. It overlooks the Port Tobacco River from Chapel Point with a spectacular view across the river. Father Andrew White, who was one of the original colonists in 1634, founded America's oldest active parish in 1641. There have been priests living at the residence for over three hundred years. The church has a piece of wood said to be from the true cross (the cross on which Christ died) brought to Maryland on *Ark* or *Dove*.

The oldest Episcopal Church in Charles County is Old Durham built in 1732. Its parish was established in 1692 at the same location.

In 1790, four Carmelite nuns founded the Mt. Carmel Monastery on Mt. Carmel Road in La Plata. This was the first monastery and the first religious community for women in the United States. The original foundation is still there.

A number of other churches dating from the 1700s are in the county, including St. Peter's Church in Waldorf (1700), Nanjemoy Baptist Church in Nanjemoy (1791), and Trinity Church in Newport (1744).

Other congregations include Amish, Apostolic, Church of Christ, Jewish, Church of God, Pentecostal, Catholic, Baptist, Presbyterian, Brethren, Episcopal, Methodist, Lutheran, AME, Unitarian Universalist, and many others.

Education and Schools

Charles County's first schools were built from a trust fund left by Maurice McDonough, an immigrant who came to this country just before the Revolutionary War. He opened a store in Pomfret and was surprised at the number of people who could not read. In his will, he provided for a trust fund that would go into effect after he and his wife died. Their property was to be sold and the money used to educate children in the area. At the time the money amounted to $3,000. In 1807, the legislature incorporated the trust and used it to build the first schools in the county. The public school system was eventually established and more schools with one or two rooms were built. The McDonough trustees then used money from the trust fund to build the McDonough Institute in La Plata around 1900. Later the public school system took over high school education, and the trust fund was also used to help students with their college education.

Sometime between 1874 and 1878, a one-room school opened in Port Tobacco for white children of farmers. It housed grades one through seven or eight. In 1928, it became a school for black children, which operated until 1954. In that year, the black children were sent to white schools as a result of the *Brown vs. Board of Education of Topeka, Kansas* decision by the Supreme Court, which ruled that separate but equal education for black children was unconstitutional (did not obey the Constitution). After that, the building was used by 4-H and boys clubs and then abandoned for a time. It was renovated over a four-year period between 1990 and 1994 and is now a museum.

Today Charles County has over 20,000 students enrolled in its schools. There is a seven-member board of education that determines educational policies and governs the county's public school system. The schools use the highest percentage of the county budget, about 54 percent. The school system also has a career and technology center, two adult education centers, an environmental education center, and an alternative school.

The College of Southern Maryland in La Plata is a two-year college. Classes are also offered in Waldorf and in Calvert and St. Mary's Counties. It was formerly known as Charles County Community College.

The University of Maryland University College offers undergraduate and graduate classes at the campus in Waldorf and specializes in adult continuing education.

Businesses, Industries, and Agriculture

Charles County has a wide variety of businesses, many located in its nine industrial parks. The county is encouraging new businesses with the availability of office, retail, and warehouse space.

Charles County's largest employer is the Naval Surface Warfare Center in Indian Head. Other large employers include Civista Medical Center, College of Southern Maryland, Automated Graphics Systems, Inc., and Southern Maryland Electric Cooperative.

Many shopping centers and malls, such as the St. Charles Town Center mall, have given Charles County the title of "shopping capital of southern Maryland." In addition, there are a number of antique stores for shoppers who want something old rather than something new.

Agriculture is a large part of Charles County's economy. Farmers grow herbs, corn, wheat, soybeans, barley, tomatoes, grapes, apples, peaches, cucumbers, potatoes, eggplant, peppers, strawberries, pumpkins, lettuce, watermelons, and many other fruits and vegetables. Some still grow tobacco. Farmers also raise cattle, horses, and goats. Canterbury's Angora Ranch raises angora rabbits.

Fascinating Folks (Past and Present)

Job Chandler was one of Charles County's first settlers. He owned land on both sides of the Port Tobacco River. He called his home Chandler's Hope.

General William Smallwood was a commander during the Revolutionary War. His troops were known as "the Maryland Line" or "the Old Liners." He rose to the rank of major general. After the war, he became governor of Maryland and served three terms.

John Hanson was the first president of the colonies under the Articles of the Confederation. A monument to him stands on the grounds of his home, Mulberry Grove, and a replica of the house has been built there. After the U.S. Constitution was ratified, George Washington became president. Historians still disagree as to who was actually the first president of the United States.

Governor William Stone was governor in 1649 when Maryland passed the Act Concerning Religion. This act guaranteed freedom of religion for all. This was the first time religious freedom had been guaranteed in America.

Thomas Stone was a signer of the Declaration of Independence. He is buried in the family graveyard at Habre de Venture in Port Tobacco.

Daniel of St. Thomas Jenifer was a signer of the Constitution of the United States in 1787. He also served as manager of state revenue. He was a delegate to Congress and a Maryland delegate to the Constitutional Convention.

Dr. James Craik, born in 1730, served with George Washington in the French and Indian War and again in the Revolutionary War. He served as surgeon general of the Continental Army. He and Washington became good friends. When Washington died in 1799, Craik was with him. Craik died in 1814.

Dr. Gustavus Richard Brown was called to George Washington's bedside during his last illness.

General James Wilkinson was born in Benedict in 1757. At nineteen, he joined the Continental Army. After the Revolution, he moved west to Kentucky where he helped persuade the Spanish to open the mouth of the Mississippi River to American trade ships. He became a

Spanish agent known as "Number Thirteen" and worked to bring the west under the control of Louisiana while also serving in the U.S. Army. In 1797, upon General Anthony Wayne's death, he took Wayne's position as commander-in-chief of the western army. In 1803, he and other commissioners accepted the transfer of land known as the Louisiana Purchase from the French. Two years later he became governor of the northern portion of that area.

During his governorship, he and Aaron Burr conspired to seize land west and south of the Louisiana Purchase from the Spanish. They tried to start another country out west, but they were not successful. Wilkinson went on to serve in the War of 1812. He was promoted to major general. He died in Mexico in 1825.

Josiah Henson was born into slavery on a farm about a mile from Port Tobacco on June 15, 1789. He had several owners during his time as a slave, and he became determined to escape. He and his family eventually escaped to Canada, where he became a minister. Henson worked to help other slaves escape. His life was the basis for Harriet Beecher Stowe's famous book *Uncle Tom's Cabin.*

Benjamin Stoddert was the first secretary of the navy appointed during the administration of President John Adams.

Ann Matthews, Susanna Matthews, Ann Theresa, and **Reverend Charles Neale** were four of the people who started the Mt. Carmel Monastery in 1790. They were natives of Charles County.

Dr. Samuel Mudd was the doctor who set John Wilkes Booth's broken leg in 1865. Booth had shot President Abraham Lincoln and was escaping from Washington with a fellow conspirator, David Herold.

NOT-SO-FUN FACT   When trying to escape, John Wilkes Booth wore a disguise and David Herold used a false name of Tyson or Tyler. Booth claimed his injury occurred when his horse fell and hurt him.

Dr. Mudd was accused of knowingly aiding a fugitive and was sentenced to life in prison. He was sent to Fort Jefferson, a prison on the Dry Tortugas islands in Florida. He was freed four years later in 1869 by President Andrew Johnson. His name has since been cleared and he is buried in St. Mary's Catholic Cemetery on Route 232.

Samuel Cox was a southern sympathizer who offered John Wilkes Booth and David Herold a hiding place in a pine forest until he could arrange for them to cross the Potomac River to Virginia.

Thomas Jones was a Confederate sympathizer from Port Tobacco who also helped the fugitives. He took food and supplies to Booth and Herold, who hid in the forest near the town for five days. On April 22, 1865, they escaped across the Potomac to Virginia in a boat Jones provided them. Jones was offered a large reward to turn in John Wilkes Booth, but he refused, saying he had given his word not to do so.

Matthew Henson was a member of Admiral Robert Peary's expedition, which made the first successful trip to the North Pole. Henson was the first black man to reach the pole. He was born in 1866 near Nanjemoy. When he was only twelve, he went to sea and spent the next six years traveling around the world as a cabin boy on a merchant ship. He met Robert Peary in a clothing store in Washington, D.C. Peary hired him to go on an expedition to Nicaragua. They became friends and shared a desire to be first to the North Pole. They made seven trips to the Arctic before they finally accomplished this. On April 6, 1909, Henson reached the site considered to be the North Pole. Peary arrived soon afterward. Thirty-six years later, Henson was awarded the Congressional Medal of Honor. Matthew Henson died in 1955. In 1961, a commemorative plaque was hung in the State House in Annapolis honoring him as a part of the team who first reached the North Pole.

Blue Dog is the ghost of a dog who is said to guard his master's gold and the deed (a paper that names the owner of a property) to his estate. The dog and his master, Charles Thomas Sims, were both killed around 1897 by Henry Hanos, who then buried the gold and the deed under a holly tree. When he came back for the treasure, Hanos was frightened by the ghost of the Blue Dog, and he died soon after. Even today people claim to see the Blue Dog.

Olivia Floyd, the owner of the property where Charles Sims and his dog were killed, first reported seeing the ghost of the Blue Dog in 1897.

FUN FACT

Natural Resources

Charles County has several wildlife areas including Mattawoman Natural Environmental Area, Zekiah Swamp, Patuxent Vista Natural Resource Management Area, and the Nanjemoy Creek Great Blue Heron Sanctuary. The county's wildlife areas have a total of 7,830 acres of forests and wetlands. Cedarville State Forest is a 3,510-acre area of forest and swamps. The headwaters of Zekiah Swamp Run are in Cedarville. The swamp run is a marshy stream that runs through bottomland swamp for twenty miles and empties into the Wicomico River. It runs through the county from the Cedarville Natural Resource Center to the headwaters of the Wicomico River.

FUN FACT   Charles County is the third most forested county in Maryland. It has the second largest population of bald eagles in the state.

There are four large rivers in Charles County, the Potomac, the Patuxent, the Wicomico, and the Port Tobacco. In addition, the county has many small rivers and numerous creeks forming approximately 150 miles of riverfront.

Places of Interest

The **Dr. Samuel A. Mudd House Museum** is located on Dr. Samuel Mudd Road near La Plata. It is the home of the doctor who set John Wilkes Booth's leg after Booth assassinated President Lincoln. The central structure of the house was built in 1754. The house is open to visitors from spring through fall three days a week.

Friendship House is a small house built by Colonel William Dent about 1680. It is one of the oldest houses still standing in Charles County. It is thought that Dent did not live there all the time but used it to help manage his estate. In 1968, the owner wanted to burn it down. The Historical Society of Charles County received permission to dismantle it. The pieces were numbered and stored for seven years while the society searched for a place to rebuild it. It was finally reconstructed on the campus of the Charles County Community College (now the

College of Southern Maryland) on Mitchell Road in La Plata. Visitors to the site can see what life was like for the early settlers.

The **General William Smallwood House Museum** in Smallwood State Park on Route 1 in Marbury is the home of the famous Revolutionary War general whose troops became known as "the Old Line." The plantation was named Smallwood Retreat and was built around 1760 just after the Revolutionary War. Tour guides in period costumes lead visitors through the house. Visitors can also see craft demonstrations and military exhibits.

The **Conoy-Piscataway Museum** on Gwinn Road in Pomonkey is a children's museum that has exhibits about Native Americans in the southern Maryland region. Visitors can see animal hides, a dugout canoe, and scenes depicting early village life.

The **Port Tobacco Historic District** on Route 6 and Chapel Point Road is one of the oldest continuously occupied areas in the southern Maryland region. Visitors can see archaeological sites and exhibits of artifacts discovered by the Society for Restoration of Port Tobacco. Visitors can also see the Stagg House, the Chimney House, and the rebuilt Port Tobacco Courthouse. The courthouse has exhibits on growing and processing tobacco. Also part of the historic district is the Catslide House on Chapel Point Road, a colonial home built in the 1720s that has hands-on activities so children can learn about the hard living conditions of the colonial era. The One-Room Schoolhouse in the historic district of Port Tobacco is also open on Wednesdays and weekends from spring to fall. Visitors can see the schoolroom just as it was when children from grades one to seven (or eight) attended.

Thomas Stone National Historic Site on Rose Hill Road in Port Tobacco was the home of Thomas Stone, a signer of the Declaration of Independence. He built the home in five sections in 1771 and called it Habre de Venture (or Haberdeventure). Part of the house burned in 1977, but it has since been rebuilt. There are farm buildings on the site from the 1800s. Stone and his wife are buried on the property.

The **American Indian Cultural Center/Piscataway Indian Museum** is located on Country Lane in Waldorf. It was established to teach people about the Piscataway Indians. The site includes a Native

American longhouse, a museum, and a library, and it shows the life of the tribe before Europeans settled in the area.

<table>
<tr><td>FUN FACT</td><td>After 1936, the paneling and corner cupboards from the first floor of Thomas Stone's home were moved to the Baltimore Museum of Art, along with family portraits.</td></tr>
</table>

The **Naval Surface Warfare Center** at Indian Head was established in 1942 in what was originally an old powder factory. This factory had opened as a proving ground in 1890. It is now involved with research, development, and manufacturing relating to "energetics," which deals with energy and its transformation. Energetics is the process that allows missiles and torpedoes to move at great speeds through air or water. The naval base has 3,500 acres of land and 1,600 buildings and employs 3,600 people. It was originally called the U.S. Propellant Plant and produced rocket fuel. The name was changed to the U.S. Naval Ordnance Station, then to the Naval Surface Warfare Center. This center has been in operation longer than any other naval ordnance center in the country.

The **Nanjemoy Creek Great Blue Heron Sanctuary,** located between Welcome and Grayton, is a busy place in mid-February. At this time nearly 2,500 great blue herons nest in the 273 acres of the sanctuary. The herons build nests in the trees and each female lays three to five eggs. These nests are counted every year to track the number of herons in the area. In the 1940s, there were about 100 nests built, but in 2000, there were 1,300, so the population is growing. The Nature Conservancy, which preserves land for wildlife, is trying to buy more land for the herons and other wildlife. The dwarf wedge mussel found in this area is found in only thirteen other places in the world.

Parks and Recreational Areas

Doncaster Forest is located on Route 6 west of La Plata. It has 1,445 acres. Visitors can hike the trails, hunt, or picnic.

Gilbert Run Park is located on Route 6 east of La Plata. It has a 60-acre freshwater lake and 180 acres of woods. Visitors can fish and go rowing or paddle-boating. Hiking the trails and picnicking are also fun in this park. It is open from early spring to late fall.

Smallwood State Park and Smallwood Retreat is a 630-acre recreational area located on Mattawoman Creek 11 miles west of La Plata. Visitors to the park can see the home of General William Smallwood, a Revolutionary War hero. Hiking and picnicking are also available in the park. The **Mattawoman Creek Art Center** is adjacent to the park. The center has art exhibits and competitions showing pottery, sculptures, and paintings.

Chapel Point State Park is located three miles south of Port Tobacco on the Port Tobacco River. In this 500-acre park visitors can enjoy fishing, hiking the trails, hunting, and exploring a historic area.

Cobb Island is located at the junction of the Potomac and Wicomico Rivers. Visitors can enjoy fishing, boating, and seafood restaurants.

Myrtle Grove Wildlife Management Area has 834 acres with a 23-acre lake and three reservoirs for fishing. It is located seven miles west of La Plata on Route 225. Visitors can enjoy birding, nature photography, hiking, a gun range, and hunting.

Chicamuxen Watchable Wildlife Center is located off Route 224 near Indian Head. Visitors can enjoy the 20 acres of wetlands formed by the Potomac River and the Chicamuxen and Mattawoman Creeks. Birders can walk the mile-long path to see a wide variety of birds, including rare ones such as the Louisiana thrush.

Friendship Farm Park and Boat Launching Facility is located on Friendship Landing Road in Nanjemoy. There are miles of scenic marshes where kayakers, canoeists, and other small boaters can enjoy the abundant wildlife. There are also many nesting sites for bald eagles. The park is open all year from dawn to dusk.

Laurel Springs Regional Park is especially fun for young children. There are sixteen athletic fields, a tot lot, a playground, a jogging trail, and two small picnic pavilions. It is located on Radio Station Road near La Plata.

Oak Ridge Park is on Oaks Road in Hughesville. There are horseback riding trails and show rings, a playground, and a picnic pavilion area.

Purse State Park on Route 224 in Indian Head has 90 acres of land and shoreline. Visitors can hunt for sharks' teeth along the shoreline.

The **Ruth B. Swann Memorial Park** is located on Bryans Road on Pomonkey Creek and the Potomac River. Visitors can hike the one-mile trail and watch the numerous birds that make their home there. There are places to picnic and play baseball and soccer.

BIBLIOGRAPHY

Arnett, Earl; Robert J. Brugger; and Edward C. Papenfuse. *Maryland, A New Guide to the Old Line State.* Baltimore: Johns Hopkins University Press, 1999.

Behrens, June, and Pauline Brower. *Colonial Farm.* Chicago: Children's Press, 1976.

Brown, Jack D. *Charles County Maryland, a History.* Hackensack: Custombook, Inc., 1976.

Carr, Lois; Russell R. Menard; and Louis Peddicord. *Maryland . . . at the Beginning.* Annapolis: Maryland State Archives, 1984, 1991.

Ferguson, Alice and Henry. *The Piscataway Indians of Southern Maryland.* Accokeek, Md.: Alice Ferguson Foundation, 1960.

Fradin, Dennis Brindell. *The Maryland Colony.* Chicago: Children's Press, 1990.

Frese, Diane P., ed. *Maryland Manual, 1994-1995.* Maryland State Archives, 1994.

Goldstein, Louis L. *Louis Goldstein's Maryland.* Annapolis, Md.: Maryland State Archives, 1985.

Hammett, Regina Combs. *History of St. Mary's County, Maryland.* Project of the St. Mary's County Bicentannial Commission, 1977.

Henson, Josiah. *An Autobiography of the Reverend Josiah Henson.* Reading, Mass.: Addison Wesley Publishing Company, 1969.

Kaminkow, Marion J. *Maryland A to Z, A Topographical Dictionary.* Baltimore: Magna Carta Book Company, 1985.

Maarck, John T. *Maryland the Seventh State, a History.* Glen Arm, Md: Creative Impressions, Ltd., 1995.

Maryland Historical and Geographic Atlas. Harford County Public Schools, revised 1995.

Roberts, Bruce and Ray Jones. *Mid-Atlantic Lighthouses, Hudson Bay to Chesapeake Bay.* Old Saybrooke, Conn.: The Globe Pequot Press, 1996.

Rollo, Vera. *The Black Experience in Maryland.* Lanham, Md.: Maryland Historical Press, 1984.

Schaun, George and Virginia. *Everyday Life in Colonial Maryland.* Lanham, Md: Maryland Historical Press, 1980.

Schaun, George and Virginia. *The Story of Early Maryland.* Annapolis, Md.: Greenbury Publications, nd.

Schmidt, Martin F. *Maryland's Geology.* Centreville, Md.: Tidewater Publishers, 1993.

Stein, Charles Francis. *A History of Calvert County, Maryland.* Baltimore: Charles L. Stein, 1976.

Tunnis, Edwin. *Shaw's Fortune.* Cleveland: World Publishing Co., 1966.

INDEX